D1518455

IMAGES OF ASIA

Old Luang Prabang

Titles in the series

Old Luang Prabang

BETTY GOSLING

KUALA LUMPUR
OXFORD UNIVERSITY PRESS
OXFORD   SINGAPORE   NEW YORK
1996

Oxford University Press

Oxford New York
Athens Auckland Bangkok Bombay
Calcutta Cape Town Dar es Salaam Delhi
Florence Hong Kong Istanbul Karachi
Madras Madrid Melbourne Mexico City
Nairobi Paris Shah Alam Singapore
Taipei Tokyo Toronto

and associated companies in
Berlin Ibadan

Oxford is a trade mark of Oxford University Press

Published in the United States
by Oxford University Press, New York

© Oxford University Press 1996
First published 1996

British Library Cataloguing in Publication Data
Data available

Library of Congress Cataloging-in-Publication Data
Gosling, Betty.
Old Luang Prabang/Betty Gosling.
p. cm. — (Images of Asia)
Includes bibliographical references and index.
ISBN 983 56 0006 6 (boards)
1. Louangphrabang (Laos)—Guidebooks. I. Title. II. Series.
DS555.98.L68G67 1996
915.94—dc20
96–14589
CIP

Typeset by Indah Photosetting Centre Sdn. Bhd., Malaysia
Printed by KHL Printing Co. (S) Pte. Ltd., Singapore
Published by the South-East Asian Publishing Unit,
a division of Penerbit Fajar Bakti Sdn. Bhd.,
under licence from Oxford University Press,
4 Jalan U1/15, Seksyen U1, 40000 Shah Alam,
Selangor Darul Ehsan, Malaysia

For Betsy

Acknowledgements

My travel to and in Laos was funded by a Luce Foundation Grant administered by the Southeast Asia Council of the Association for Asian Studies. I am grateful also to Dr John Whitmore of the University of Michigan for taking time to read my manuscript, to share his interest and enviable knowledge, and to offer invaluable advice. Professor Bill Gedney, as always, has been generous with his explanations of Tai words.

Ann Arbor   BETTY GOSLING
September 1995

Contents

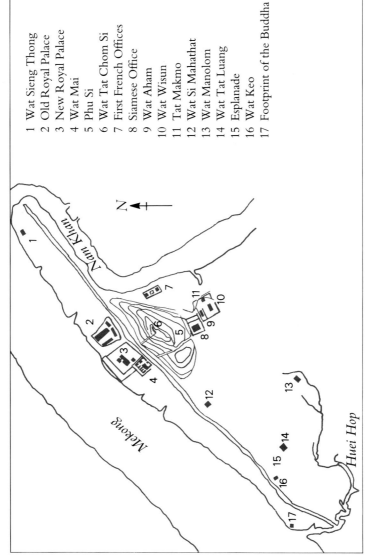

1 Wat Sieng Thong
2 Old Royal Palace
3 New Royal Palace
4 Wat Mai
5 Phu Si
6 Wat Tat Chom Si
7 First French Offices
8 Siamese Office
9 Wat Aham
10 Wat Wisun
11 Tat Makmo
12 Wat Si Mahathat
13 Wat Manolom
14 Wat Tat Luang
15 Esplanade
16 Wat Keo
17 Footprint of the Buddha

Map 1. Map of Luang Prabang

1
The Setting

COMPARED with other capital cities of the world, Luang Prabang, the royal capital of Laos, is not the most ancient, nor is it anywhere near the largest or the most famous. Until the latter half of the nineteenth century, the royal city, secluded in the forested, mountainous northern regions of what is now the Lao People's Democratic Republic, was a mystery to most of the world beyond, a very small place in the last area in all of Asia to be reached by European explorers. Even today, in the last decade of the twentieth century, when South-East Asia has become a major focus of foreign interest, Luang Prabang remains remote, pristine, and detached from the modern world, a city whose royal identity rests as much on myth and time-honoured ritual as recorded history.

The most densely populated part of the old capital occupies a hilly area bordered on the west by the turbulent Mekong, South-East Asia's longest river, which cascades from the mountains of Tibet into the South China Sea, 4000 kilometres away; on the east flows the more placid Nam Khan, one of the Mekong's many tributaries (Map 1). The rivers converge at the northern tip of the settlement to form a narrow peninsula that broadens as the Nam Khan meanders towards the south-east.

Although Luang Prabang spreads some distance beyond its riverbanks, its major thoroughfare stretches for 3 kilometres from the tip of the peninsula to a small stream, the Huei Hop, which functions as the city's southern boundary. Most of the buildings line the thoroughfare, clustering near a steep and forested hill, Phu Si—the Sacred Mount—that abuts the road near the centre of the peninsula. At the summit of Phu Si, a Buddhist stupa, Tat Chom Si (Colour Plate 1), towers majestically above the streets and houses below and dominates the countryside beyond (Plate 1). Nestled among its hills and rivers and rapids, the city has retained a natural and man-made charm that is unique. Its setting is renowned not

1. Luang Prabang as seen from across the Nam Khan: in the centre, the sacred hill, Phu Si, and Tat Chom Si. (From a woodblock print by Louis Delaporte, in Garnier, 1873, Vol. 1)

only for its tranquillity and solitude but also for its grandeur and beauty.

Luang Prabang is much more than a scenic delight, however, for it is also the ancient home of Laos's first monarchs, the birthplace of a united Laotian people. The city's local name, 'Muang Luang', or royal city-state, reflects that status. Similarly, the city's official title, Nakhon Luang Prabang, identifies it as the royal city of the Pra Bang, a golden image of the Buddha (Plate 2) whose magical powers for five centuries, it was thought, protected the city and its kingdom from harm. From time to time since Luang Prabang's historical founding in the mid-fourteenth century, a larger and more centrally located Laotian city, Vientiane, 225 kilometres to the south, has served as the country's administrative capital, as it has in the twentieth century. But nothing has replaced Luang Prabang's imperial designation. Although no king has reigned at the old capital since 1975, when the monarchy was abolished and the kingdom was politically restructured as a socialist republic, the city's royal identity remains unshaken.

Both Luang Prabang's idyllic setting and its official title are deceiving, however, for if one looks beneath the surface, one finds a turbulent history of wars, invasions, and conquests that is anything but peaceful and regnally secure. If the city's isolation from non-Asian countries led to the preservation of its natural and cultural beauties, its involvement with lands nearby produced an extraordinary history in which political alliances were frequently reconfigured and territories wavered, evaporated, and re-emerged in unpredictable patterns.

Luang Prabang's geographical situation was pivotal (Map 2). Its territories to the west (now, north-east Thailand) could be reached by elephant-back across an especially shallow stretch of the Mekong, and further to the south-west, travel by bullock cart, elephant-back, and boat along the Nan and Chao Phraya Rivers connected the royal city with Nan, Phichai, and Bangkok. A few kilometres upstream from Luang Prabang, two navigable tributaries of the Mekong, the Nam Ou and the Nam Seuang, like the Nam Khan, which flowed into the city itself, led to the north-eastern regions of Vietnam.

2. The Pra Bang Buddha image. (From
Thongsa, n.d.)

The confluence of the rivers created flat lands that produced rice
crops more than sufficient to meet the needs of the local people, a
rare occurrence along the middle stretches of the Mekong. Moreover, there was benzoin, a resin used in medicines and perfumes, for
export; and stick-lac, deposited by insects on the flame-of-the-forest
trees that grew on the rivers' flood-plains, was also in demand for
varnishes and dyes. Trade among the mountain peoples in the
northern part of Laos, the Vietnamese of Tonkin, and the Lu of
southern China, was lively. Caravans of traders arrived from as far
away as Dali, in western Yunnan, with carpets and textiles from
China and Tibet, and traders from Burma (Myanmar) brought
ceramic and metal wares (Plate 3).

Map 2. Mainland South-East Asia (with twentieth-century political boundaries)

3. The multi-ethnic market at Luang Prabang in 1867. (From a woodblock print by Louis Delaporte, in Garnier, 1873, Vol. 2)

The areas over which Luang Prabang exercised political control fluctuated wildly. At times, its territories included parts of what are now north-west Thailand and southern China; in less prosperous times, on four occasions, the city was plundered by Vietnamese, Lao, and Chinese troops (in 1478, 1707, 1791, and 1887). In the late nineteenth century the country was split in two by an arbitrary boundary line (the Mekong), dividing it between Siam and France; and for a decade and a half—from 1893 to 1907—the old capital itself was thus divided. Far from being the isolated spot that Westerners usually envision, Luang Prabang was, for most of its history, complexly involved in the affairs of its neighbours, both friendly and hostile (Pavie et al., Vol. 1, p. 209; Vol. 3, p. 34; Vol. 5, pp. 88–91; Vol. 6, p. 32).

How was the city able to maintain both its silvan beauty and its royal identity despite the complexities and entanglements that its geographical and historical circumstances presented? And why, located on the banks of one of the world's longest rivers at the centre of South-East Asia's major nations, has it remained comparatively unchanged and little known to the outside world?

Those questions evoke some of the most fascinating tales in South-East Asia's history. To find the answers, one must delve into the ancient past—a past that began long before there was a written language to record it and which was kept alive by means of legend, myth, and ritual. At Luang Prabang—the royal city of the Pra Bang—myth and history, the sacred and the secular, the ceremonial and the ordinary blended and fused, and thereby its status was maintained. Only when one contemplates those age-old beliefs and traditions can the royal city be understood as it exists in the present.

2
Luang Prabang in Myth and History

ACCORDING to Lao mythology, long before the earth was inhabited by people, it was covered with primeval forests that were populated by multitudinous *phi*—spirits of the mountains, rivers, trees, and streams—and marvellous, semi-divine ogres and demons with magical powers who jealously protected their territories. The celestial region was the home of even greater divinities—human-like beings whose miraculous powers were more potent than the spirits who guarded the earth. At that time, earth and heaven were not separated as they are today, and it was not uncommon for the heavenly gods to descend to earth and claim parts of it for them-selves. Then, in order to ensure the protection and prosperity of their newly acquired lands, the celestial gods had to placate and propitiate the earthly ones whose territories they had invaded (Pavie, 1898; Finot, 1917; de Berval, 1959, pp. 379–410).

Such is the mythological background of the founding of Laos and of the dynasty that would rule the country from its royal city, Luang Prabang, until the mid-twentieth century. According to the legends, the Lao kings were descended from the king of the heav-enly gods, Khun Borom, who, wishing to conquer the earthly re-gions, descended from the sky on his royal elephant with tusks that crossed each other and landed at a place called Muang Then (City of the Gods), later known as Dien Bien Phu, in north-western Vietnam. From there, Khun Borom, bearing his royal insignia, made his way through the inhospitable forests and its spirits. Accompanying him were two servants, Pu No and Na No, who, equipped with shovels, hoes, and axes, demolished the earthly ve-getation and any hostile peoples who hindered their progress (Plate 4). When the royal party reached what would later become Luang Prabang, Pu No and Na No became the future city's *devata luang*, or royal tutelary gods, more powerful by far than the fifteen *naga* (serpent deities) that had previously protected the area. The

4. One of Luang Prabang's *devata luang*, Pu No and
   Na No, as portrayed by a mid-twentieth century-
   ceremonial dancer. (From Sarraut, 1930)

eldest son of Khun Borom, Khun Lo (according to the myths) became Luang Prabang's first king, and thereby, the progenitor of the
royal Lao dynasty that would rule Laos until the mid-twentieth
century.

As fanciful as the mythological accounts of the founding of
Luang Prabang are, parallels between the legends and historical
facts are not entirely absent. A location near Dien Bien Phu, where
Khun Borom is said to have descended to earth, is now considered
by linguists and some historians to have been the birthplace of the

5. Wood and thatched house, northern Laos. (From a woodblock print by Louis Delaporte, in Garnier, 1873, Vol. 1)

Tai people (of whom the Lao are a major branch) and who, in the early years of the second millennium AD, began to leave the regions around Muang Then to found new *muang*, or city-states, throughout much of mainland South-East Asia.

The Tai, whether they settled in what is now Thailand, or southern China, or Laos, were an agricultural people whose subsistence depended on the cultivation of wet rice, vegetables, and buffaloes that were used for tilling the soil. The Tai lived in wood and thatch houses built high off the ground on stilts (Plate 5), and their gods—like those in Luang Prabang's time-honoured legends—were the gods of the forests and rivers and mountains. Like the guardians Pu No and Na No, the Lao who arrived at Luang Prabang had to free their new land from its former inhabitants, known in Lao as Kha (LeBar and Suddard, 1960, pp. 36, 42, and 202). The Lao pushed the Kha from the fertile valleys to the less hospitable hillsides where they practised slash-and-burn agriculture, hunting, and gathering, thereby distinguishing them from

10

the Lao wet-rice growers on the river plains. The identity of the Kha was also preserved in Luang Prabang's richly constructed mythological and ceremonial life.

Far more important than any historical information that the Lao myths and rites can provide, however, is the crucial role they played in the establishment and perpetuation of Luang Prabang as the Royal City. That does not mean that the myths were never altered. From at least as early as the eleventh century, Luang Prabang had been in close touch with the powerful Khmer Empire that ruled from Angkor, in Cambodia. And from the Khmer, the Lao learned of the ancient Indian religions, Hinduism and Buddhism, whose beliefs sometimes slipped unobtrusively into the traditional mythology. Thus, Khun Borom was sometimes identified with the Indian king of the gods, Indra; and Khun Borom's magnificent elephant, on which he had descended to earth in formidable majesty, was sometimes equated with Indra's royal mount, the 33-headed elephant, Erawan. Some of the *phi* were transformed into *devata*, minor tutelary gods in the Indian pantheon, whose purpose, like that of the guardian *phi*, was to protect the land and its people. But the old mythological framework was never shaken. As a belief system, it provided a unifying world-view, a foundation on which Luang Prabang's royal status and the ethnic identity of its people, the Lao and the Kha, were based.

By the end of the thirteenth century, the history of Luang Prabang began to be recorded in historical sources. Then, as recorded in a 1292 Siamese stone inscription, Luang Prabang, known by an earlier name, Muang Sawa, was one of many small principalities that paid tribute to Sukhothai, the most powerful *muang* in what would later become central Thailand (Griswold and Prasert, 1971, pp. 179–228). By the mid-fourteenth century, with Luang Prabang's first historically documented king, Fa Ngum, on the throne, historical accounts began to be preserved at Luang Prabang as well (Le Boulanger, 1934; LeBar and Suddard, 1960; Hall, 1964; Wyatt, 1982).

Fa Ngum was not an ordinary Lao, for he had been reared in the royal court of Angkor and had married a daughter of the Khmer king. From that prestigious base, in 1353, Fa Ngum fought his way

11

up the Mekong valley and, with the help of his Khmer father-in-law, united a number of small semi-independent *muang* in what is now northern Laos. Thus was founded the first Lao kingdom, called Lan Sang, the Land of the Million Elephants, with its capital at Muang Sawa, sometimes called by its local name, Sieng Dong-Sieng Thong and, two centuries later, Luang Prabang.

Like the rulers of many of the lands nearby, Fa Ngum officially espoused Theravada Buddhism as a means of unifying his territories politically. Unlike the old indigenous myths that were understood locally, the Theravada religion provided a system of beliefs that was shared by peoples throughout South-East Asia. The newly adopted faith was a religion of the people and it served to bind people, king, and the Buddhist monkhood into a cohesive structure that went beyond specific localities. From Angkor, King Fa Ngum received the golden image of the Buddha called Pra Bang (Plates 2 and 6), which eventually would become the royal palladium of the Lao kingdom, a more powerful guardian than the *devata luang*, Pu No and Na No (Lingat, 1934, pp. 9–38).

The Pra Bang arrived at Luang Prabang with a mythology all its own and very different from the old indigenous ones. According to the legends of the Pra Bang, the image was made in Sri Lanka, the homeland of Theravada Buddhism, where the Sinhalese king, the Lord Indra, various Brahmins, a few ascetics, and numerous *deva* helped with the casting. The people of Sri Lanka had collected gold, silver, copper, and brass, which was dropped into a pot of molten metal, and when it was completed, the image was said to have had such magical power that everyone came to worship it. After many generations, the king of Cambodia, wishing to associate himself with the Theravada religion of Sri Lanka, asked the Sinhalese king for the image, and after many more years, the Khmer king sent it as a gift to Fa Ngum, his son-in-law and king of the Lao, ruling at Luang Prabang. The golden image portrayed the Buddha standing with both arms raised forward at the elbows, palms facing outward. The image was not particularly large—50 centimetres tall—but its genealogy was unsurpassed and the *mudra* (hand-gesture) signified assurance that the image would offer protection to those who honoured it.

6. The Pra Bang image ceremonially displayed in a *prasat*. At upper right, the head of the *hanglin* by means of which the image was aspersed. (From Marchal, 1964, Vol. 10, No. 2)

In spite of the strong impact that Theravada Buddhism was making on Luang Prabang, however, the Pra Bang also embodied old indigenous beliefs. For, it was thought, the image was inhabited by a vigorous and lively *phi*, who from time to time (as will be made clear below), made its presence brazenly felt. Luang Prabang's history proved to be tumultuous, and it used all the symbols it could muster. Not only did the Pra Bang unite Luang Prabang's royal and religious realms, but also its indigenous and Buddhist beliefs.

7. Street scene with the monastery Wat Mai in 1867. (From a wood-block print by Louis Delaporte, in Garnier, 1873, Vol. 2)

The Pra Bang appears to have had a propitious influence at Luang Prabang from the beginning. Fa Ngum, by means of his warlike practices (more than his Buddhist piety, one might guess), expanded his territories, which, by the end of his reign, in 1373, included not only a major portion of what is now Laos, but also large parts of northern Siam (now Thailand) and Vietnam. By the end of Fa Ngum's reign, the territories, though sparsely populated, made up one of the largest principalities in South-East Asia.

Under Fa Ngum's son, King Sam Saen Tai, who ruled from 1373 until 1416, Luang Prabang continued to flourish. Sam Saen Tai was a more peaceful ruler than his father, and he promoted the study of Buddhism, built temples, and founded monasteries, or *wat*, for the ever-growing number of Theravada monks (Plate 7). By peaceful means, he consolidated many of the small Lao *muang* that previously had been only loosely associated with one another;

he founded a more cohesive administrative structure; and by means of a complex military organization, he maintained peace and stability. But the kings who followed Sam Saen Tai were not so successful, and many of their reigns were brief. In 1478, Luang Prabang was captured and occupied for a short time by Vietnamese troops, an event that foretold the almost incessant conflict between Laos and its neighbours that would plague the city in the following centuries.

In the past, Luang Prabang's closest ties had been with the north; by the sixteenth century, however, areas further to the south were gaining in importance, and Luang Prabang was losing its favourable geographic position. Warfare was rampant: there were wars with Vietnam, Cambodia, Lan Na (northern Thailand), Ava (in Burma), and among the Lao themselves. In 1527, Luang Prabang's King Photthisarat (r. 1520–47) left Luang Prabang and took up residence in Vientiane, in central Laos, and soon his son, Setthathirat, was ruling from Chiang Mai, the capital of Lan Na. Luang Prabang was left more and more in the background.

It was during this period, however, that a large number of Theravada Buddhist monks began journeying to Luang Prabang from Cambodia and Siam to study. Many more temples were built at the old capital (Plate 8); and while Vientiane busied itself with political matters, Luang Prabang became an important centre of Buddhist learning. When, in 1563, King Setthathirat officially moved his capital from Luang Prabang to Vientiane, there were efforts to preserve the older capital's royal status: it was then that Muang Sawa's name was changed to Luang Prabang, the Royal City of the Pra Bang.

Relations between the old and new capitals were far from mutually supportive, and rivalry for prestige and power between them was more common than not. During the latter half of the sixteenth century and throughout the seventeenth, the dichotomy resulted in numerous confrontations among many factions, rulers, and territories, and matters went from bad to worse. In 1707, after years of warfare, Luang Prabang and Vientiane became entirely separate—rival kingdoms, divided by mutual hostility. Vientiane

8. The *sim* at Wat Sieng Thong with monks. (From Pavie et al., Vol. 3)

was for the time being the winner, and the Pra Bang was moved south from Luang Prabang to the more centrally located capital, Vientiane.

With the loss of its palladium and its status as royal capital of a united kingdom, Luang Prabang's decline was exacerbated. Warfare with Vientiane continued, and by the mid-eighteenth century, there appeared an even greater threat, this time from the west: Siam. The Siamese, playing Luang Prabang and Vientiane against each other in order to control them both, provoked incessant warfare. In 1778, Siamese troops captured the Pra Bang, still in Vientiane, and carted it off to Thonburi, at that time the Siamese capital across the Chao Phraya River from Bangkok. By the end of the eighteenth century, most of Laos was under some form of Siamese control and would remain so until the French established a protectorate there a century later.

Although it is difficult for modern historians to be very concerned with any role the Pra Bang may have played in Laos's and Luang Prabang's political history, to both the Lao and the Siamese, ownership of the image was a serious matter, and their opinions are worth mentioning. When the Pra Bang arrived in Thonburi in

1778, it was accompanied by a second image, the Pra Keo, which had been brought to Luang Prabang, and later, to Vientiane from Chiang Mai in the sixteenth century. When the two images arrived in Thonburi, they were welcomed ceremoniously, ritually installed in a temple especially built for them in the precincts of the royal palace, and there they were worshipped together as proclamation of Siam's suzerainty over Lan Sang. When in 1781, Siam's Rama I (King Ramathibodhi) moved the Siamese capital across the Chao Phraya River from Thonburi to Bangkok, the two images were moved to the new Royal Chapel, where the Pra Keo remains today as the palladium of the modern nation, Thailand.

The Pra Bang was not to remain nearly so long, however. Four years after its arrival, in 1782, a prince of Lan Sang journeyed to Bangkok and demanded its return, an event detailed in Bangkok's Royal Chronicles. According to the Chronicles, the Lao prince proclaimed to the Siamese officials that the installation of the Pra Bang and the Pra Keo in the same city could only lead to a great many problems. Like the Pra Bang, the Pra Keo was inhabited by a powerful *phi*, and it was the prince's opinion that there was such rivalry and hatred between the two spirits that keeping them near each other would be disastrous. As the Lao prince pointed out, while the Pra Keo had resided in Chiang Mai, before its removal to Luang Prabang, Lan Sang had been thriving and happy. But after the Pra Keo had been transported to Luang Prabang, where the Pra Bang still dwelt, serious troubles befell the kingdom; and when the two images were brought to Vientiane, the kingdom deteriorated even further. With the two images in Thonburi, matters were indeed terrible: the Siamese King Taksin went mad; rebels seized his palace; and political upheavals plagued the entire country. Hearing this, and in order to forestall additional troubles, Rama I, in 1782, dispatched the Pra Bang from Bangkok back to its former home in Vientiane.

That was not the end of the rivalry between the Pra Keo and the Pra Bang, however. Following years of warfare between Laos and Siam, Siamese troops, in 1728, delivered their most devastating blow: the Siamese attacked Vientiane, destroying everything in the city but its Buddhist temples, and the Pra Bang was carried off once again to Bangkok. Again, the Pra Bang made its hostility towards the Pra Keo manifest in no uncertain terms, and once more, the troubles were recounted in Bangkok's Royal Chronicles.

In 1828, the reigning monarch of Siam was Rama III, and well aware of the problems that were thought to have resulted from the proximity of the Pra Bang and the Pra Keo in the previous century, the king placed the Pra Bang in a royal temple that had been built for it alone, outside the city. Apparently the distance between it and the Pra Keo was not enough, however. When disasters arose half a century later, the Siamese were quick to blame the Pra Bang for their problems. During the years 1865, 1866, and 1867, Siam experienced the worst droughts that anyone could remember, each year worse than the preceding one. Rice harvests were seriously affected, and the price of food rose to heights unlike anything since the founding of Bangkok. Responding to a petition signed by his ministers of state, Siam's Rama IV (King Mongkut), in 1867, arranged for the return of the Pra Bang to what he considered to be its rightful home, Luang Prabang, where it had been officially received half a millennium before (Flood, 1966, pp. 470–9; Flood and Flood, 1978, pp. 33–4).

A Lao official escorted the statue overland across the Khorat plateau to the royal city of the Pra Bang, where, on the banks of the Mekong, it was displayed for seven days and seven nights on the embarcadero. A great festival was held in the presence of all the royal court, and then the image was moved to the site of the royal palace. But, although the Lao king, Tiantha, immediately demanded that a new temple be built to house the image, the *phi* said to inhabit it apparently still did not feel compensated for his lengthy exile in Bangkok. The new temple burned before it was completed, and when instead, in 1887, the Pra Bang was moved to a former abode, Luang Prabang's Wat Wisun, that monastery too was destroyed.

The history of the Pra Bang in the twentieth century is no less intriguing than its history in more remote times. By the late nineteenth century, Europeans were beginning to come to Laos, and in 1867, the year of the Pra Bang's ceremonious return to Luang Prabang from Bangkok, a contingent of French colonialists also arrived at the Royal City. In 1893, five years after the Pra Bang was returned to its former home at Wat Wisun, French rule replaced the old Siamese regime. The French, like the Pra Bang, would remain in Luang Prabang until the mid-twentieth century, when new political upheavals ravaged the country.

Before those stories are told, however, it is necessary to look more carefully at the political and ritual make-up of Luang Prabang as it existed before the Europeans arrived.

3

The Royal City: Its Shrines and Temples

IT was not only the Pra Bang and the territorial spirit thought to
inhabit it that contributed to the perpetuation of Luang Prabang's
royal status. The city itself was in fact a ceremonial centre as much
as a political and economic one, and its prosperity was sustained by
complexly structured rituals as much as by mundane enterprise. At
one time the city supported well over fifty shrines and temples
where the city's ceremonial life transpired. The histories and legends that surround the sacred sites were intricately intertwined
with the history—mythological and real—of the city itself.

In the beginning, before the introduction of Buddhism, natural
landmarks defined the city's ceremonial topography. Specified
rocks and caverns along the river-banks were the abodes of fifteen
naga (serpent deities), who controlled the flow of the waters
necessary for the production of rice, the staple food on which the
Lao depended for their subsistence. At the summit of the hill that
rose majestically at the centre of the city (where a Buddhist stupa
would later be built), lived an especially powerful *naga* who ruled
the others (see Finot, 1917; *Le Laos*, 1967; Archaimbault, 1972 and
1973).

Not surprisingly, the legends that told of the founding of the
city also focused on its natural features. According to one story,
Muang Sawa, as Luang Prabang was then known, was founded by
two holy men, hermits, who, like visitors arriving at the city in
much later times, were impressed by the steep and verdant hill at
the centre of the peninsula that was formed by the two great rivers.
The holy men thought that the hill resembled a huge pile of rice,
and equally auspicious, they thought, was a magnificent flame-of-
the-forest tree (*thon thong*) that grew at the confluence of the rivers.
The amazing tree, we are told, was 234 metres high, 34 metres in
circumference, and bore flowers and fruits as red as lac.

Believing the site to be favourable for the founding of a city, the two holy men planted its foundation stones: one at the foot of the giant flame-tree; one near a stream called Nam Dong (south of Luang Prabang's present city limits); one to the east, in what was later to be known as the rice-fields of the gods; and one at the centre of the city, at the summit of the hill that looked like a heap of rice (later to be named Phu Si). The hermits then convened the fifteen *naga* and admonished them to guard the new *muang*: now the serpents were guardians of the political realm as well as the rice-fields. The holy men changed the old name of the city from Muang Sawa to Sieng Dong-Sieng Thong—'Sieng' meaning 'city'; 'Dong' alluding to the stream south of the city; and 'Thong' referring to the *thon thong*, or flame-of-the-forest tree at the northern tip of the city. On the stone at the foot of the flame-tree there was a message: 'In this place will be erected the palace of the monarch who in future times will reign at the city.'

Eventually, altars dedicated to the city's protector deities were built throughout the city, and there the spirits were propitiated with offerings of candles and food. The old tutelary shrines were smaller versions of the houses that people lived in (see Plate 5): simple huts, 2 or 3 metres high and 1 to 2 metres wide, constructed of wood, bamboo, and thatch, and raised high off the ground on poles. After Theravada Buddhism had been introduced, Buddhist temples were built on the sites of the old shrines.

The Buddhist temples did not look like the old stilted spirit shrines, however: like religious buildings in Cambodia, Luang Prabang's Buddhist structures were large and imposing and built flat on the ground. In place of a single offertory shrine, several types of buildings were built within a monastery complex surrounded by a high wall or fence (Plate 9). The largest building in the compound was the congregation hall, or *sim* (Plate 10; Colour Plates 4 and 5), in which numerous images of the Buddha, large and small, were placed on altars located at one end of the assembly hall; numerous small chapels housed single Buddha images (Colour Plates 6 and 7). There were also solid masonry structures—stupas, in Laos known as *tat*—to enshrine relics (material remains) of important religious or royal personages (see Colour Plates 5–7). The more important monasteries had libraries to store Buddhist texts.

21

9. Monastery with a congregation hall, or *sim* (*left*) and a stupa, or *tat* (*right*). (From a woodblock print by Louis Delaporte, in Garnier, 1873, Vol. 1)

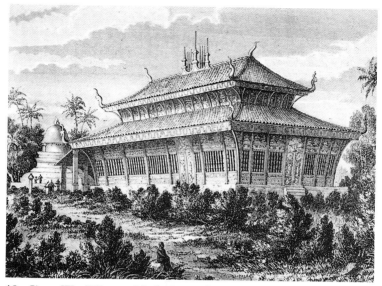

10. *Sim* at Wat Wisun, with sloping walls and *dok so fa*. (From a woodblock print by Louis Delaporte, in Garnier, 1873, Vol. 1)

In order to protect the palm-leaf manuscripts from dampness and insects, the libraries, like the old earth shrines, were raised off the ground (Plate 11).

Luang Prabang's *sim* were especially grand and ornate. Some of the monks who built the temples were accomplished architects and sculptors, specialists in ivory, wood, gold, or silver, and their *sim*, both in their interiors and exteriors, were palatial in their elaborate ornamentation (Pavie et al., Vol. 6, p. 228) (Plate 12). The *sim* were also elaborately furnished: a nineteenth-century account noted that in one monastery (Wat Wisun) the *sim* was provided with 'votive offerings of very great value, parasols, embroidered banners, and bronze statues; the most curious and richest of these objects', the account continues, were 'two elephant tusks of incomparable size', 1.85 metres and 1.65 metres long, 'covered from top to bottom with original sculptures and gilded with remarkable skill' (Garnier, 1873, Vol. 1, p. 326).

11. Library in a Buddhist monastery, northern Laos.
(From a woodblock print by Louis Delaporte, in
Garnier, 1873, Vol. 1)

The architect–monks worked in a style later to be typified as
northern Lao. The walls of the *sim*, the chapels, and libraries leaned
outward toward the roof–line, and along with the representations
of Buddhist *devata* (see Colour Plates 2, 3, and 15) similar to those
found on the doorways and walls of Theravada buildings throughout South-East Asia, the walls of Luang Prabang's monastery buildings were carved with distinctive vegetal motifs (see Colour Plate 3).
Also notable was the *dok so fa*, an ornate metal device said to sym-
bolize the universe, which rose from the centre of the *sim*'s roof
(see Plates 8 and 10).

Like stupas in other parts of Laos, Luang Prabang's *tat* had un-
usual domes in the shape of a carafe. But occasionally there were

12. Lacquer chest used for storing Buddhist manuscripts at Wat Wisun. The design depicting Buddhist *deva* is painted in gold. (From Marchal, 1964, Vol. 10, No. 2)

designs imported from neighbouring countries. Decorative green ceramic tiles on the base of Tat Luang (Colour Plate 8), dating from the period of Siamese political control, reflect a nineteenth-century Bangkok style. The *tat* at Wat Si Mahatat (Colour Plate 9), built in 1548, when Prince Setthathirat was ruling from Chiang Mai, was built as a stupa-*prasat* (cubicle base surmounted by a stupa), in the Lan Na style.

Theravada Buddhism, like the cult of the earth spirits, was a popular religion, and the *wat* were meant to be frequented by laymen as well as the monkhood. The *sim* were designed to accommodate large groups of devotees, and the grounds were spacious. While the Theravada monks, clad in saffron robes, dyed various shades of yellow, orange, and rust, studied their religious texts, performed their ritual duties, and tended their courtyards, the lay people congregated in the *sim* to meditate, to make offerings of food, incense, and flowers to the Buddha images, and to listen to the monks who chanted the Buddhist texts. In addition, the *wat* functioned as a community centre where people gathered to socialize and enjoy themselves. Within the monastery compounds the affairs of everyday life merged with the Buddhist rites that were enacted in the *sim* and the even older religious traditions that had sanctified the sites long before the monasteries were built.

* * *

Like the city itself, Luang Prabang's most important monasteries have both real life and mythological histories which, combined with archaeological data, have much to say about how Luang Prabang developed and functioned as a royal city. Nine of the city's *wat* can be singled out as especially important in terms of their historical and ritual significance, and these are described briefly below (see Finot, 1917, pp. 5–9; Parmentier, 1954, pp. 48–79 and 157–71).

Wat Sawankhalok. Situated near the confluence of the Mekong and a stream, the Nam Dong, several kilometres south of Luang Prabang's present-day city limits, Wat Sawankhalok is believed to occupy the earliest Buddhist site at Luang Prabang (Levy, 1940, pp. 411–28). Five stone Buddha images and a long inscription that were discovered in and near the *wat* indicate that two centuries before the arrival of Fa Ngum and the founding of the Theravada branch of Buddhism the site was occupied by a flourishing Khmer settlement, an extension of the powerful kingdom ruled from Angkor, in Cambodia. The Sawankhalok Buddha images reflect the Mahayana branch of Buddhism that was royally supported at Angkor in the eleventh and twelfth centuries and portray the Buddha seated beneath the multi-headed *naga*, Mucalinda, who, according to Buddhist doctrines, protected the Buddha-to-be just before his enlightenment. Serpent deities played a major role in the mythology of Angkor, as they did in Luang Prabang, and it is not surprising that the *naga*-protected Buddha image was a popular iconographic form in both areas.

A Theravada monastery was built at Sawankhalok by King Photthisarat in 1527, but was badly damaged in a hailstorm in 1883. Although the present *sim* was not built until 1905, it was still, in the mid-twentieth century, one of Luang Prabang's most ritually important sites.

Wat Keo. In 1353, when Luang Prabang's first historically documented king, Fa Ngum, took the throne, a new contingent of Khmer monks, this time of the Theravada school, arrived at Luang Prabang from Angkor and settled near the mouth of the Huei Hop, a small tributary of the Mekong north of the older Mahayana settlement. Near the confluence of the rivers, on a rock where one of the city's fifteen *naga* protectors was said to have dwelt, a footprint of the Buddha was found, thereby providing testimony that the *naga* had agreed to the Khmer monks' request for permission to build their monastery on the old *naga*-protected territories. The Khmer contingent was said to have included a large number of monks, artisans, and learned men, as well as a set of the Tripitaka, a collection of texts that make up the Theravada canon. The arrival of the Khmer traditionally marks the official introduction of Buddhism into Lan Sang (de Berval, 1959, pp. 391–410).

According to other accounts, the Buddha statue Pra Bang was also brought by the Khmer contingent. Although it is often assumed that the Pra Bang image was installed in the Wat Keo *sim*, there is no evidence of that, and more than likely, as the palladium of the kingdom, it was housed in the royal palace, where it provided legitimation to the king and his role as protector of the land and the Buddhist community.

The Wat Keo *sim* was destroyed by fire in 1883 and was not rebuilt, but its location has not been forgotten. A worn remnant of the Buddha's footprint on the rock near the mouth of the Huei Hop was still visible in the early twentieth century, and a few examples of Khmer stone sculpture of a decadent style typical of fourteenth-century Angkorean art have been found. That style did not spread or persist, however; it has been seen only in the vicinity of Wat Keo.

Wat Manolom. Although Wat Manolom is reported to have been built by Fa Ngum's son, Sam Saen Tai, in 1372, only a quarter century after the founding of Wat Keo, and although it is located not far from the older monastery, the old Khmer style of sculpture was not incorporated. What has surprised and puzzled art historians is the presence of a huge Buddha image, not in the style of the Khmer stone images found nearby, but in the Thai Sukhothai bronze tradition of the late fourteenth century (Plate 13). The image, as described in the Wat Keo chronicle, was cast in bronze in the early 1370s and was 6 metres high. It was from this style that the Lao sculptural art style has been handed down until the present day (Parmentier, 1954, pp. 281–3).

The much smaller Pra Bang image was moved to Wat Manolom, presumably from the royal palace, in 1502 and remained there until 1513, when it was moved once again, this time to Wat Wisun (described below). The Manolom *sim* underwent reconstruction in 1818, burned in 1887, and was rebuilt once again in 1972.

Wat Tat Luang. Wat Tat Luang, Monastery of the Royal Stupa, is also located in the southern part of the city and perhaps derives some of its prestige from its proximity to the older monasteries. Remnants of stone Buddha images found in its precincts and dated by art historians to the early twelfth century were perhaps brought from the old Khmer site at Sawankhalok. The *sim* was said to have been built from branches of the *bodhi* tree which had been planted near Wat Keo.

More important than the *wat's* local history, however, was a much more complex one that combined elements of pre-Buddhist, Buddhist, and royal traditions with roots far distant from Luang Prabang. According to its mythology (for which there is no historical evidence), Wat Tat Luang (see Colour Plate 8) was built by missionaries sent from India by the great Buddhist king, Asoka, in the third century BC and was known also as the Si Dharma Asoka

13. Colossal bronze image of the Buddha, dated to the 1370s, as it appeared in the early twentieth century after the destruction of the *sim* at Wat Manolom. (From Sarraut, 1930)

Stupa (Revered Stupa of Asoka and the Buddhist Law). Some accounts of the legend claim that it was Asoka himself who founded the monastery. In either case, the stories go, after the Buddha had died and passed into nirvana, some of his relics were deposited at various sites in Laos that had already been made holy by some

29

previous local tradition. At Luang Prabang, the relics were said to have been deposited in a sacred grove of lime trees inhabited by an ogre, Nang Kang Hi, where Tat Luang would be built.

Tat Luang was located on an expansive open field, or esplanade, where annual ceremonies and royal cremations were held, and the site was for many centuries the most ritually important—in terms of Buddhist, pre-Buddhist, and royal beliefs—in all of Luang Prabang (Chapter 4, below).

Wat Wisun. Located on the site where the legendary holy men were said to have laid one of the city's boundary stones, Wat Wisun (see Plate 10) is also said to have been built on the rice-fields of the city's two major tutelary spirits, Pu No and Na No. Still other accounts contend that, in order to sanctify the land, the Buddha himself planted the foundation stone so that a temple would be built there in the future by a pious and noble king. It was King Photthisarat who, in honour of his father, King Wisun, fulfilled that prophecy in 1513 with mammoth timbers provided by Luang Prabang's tributary states and shipped down the Mekong from the northern provinces.

Wat Wisun was also the site of one of Luang Prabang's most impressive stupas, Tat Makmo, with a rounded dome stylistically more Sinhalese than Lao (Colour Plate 10). The stupa was filled with images of the Buddha, many of which were carried off by Chinese raiders in 1887, when both the *sim* and the *tat* were destroyed. After being rebuilt in 1898, the *tat* collapsed once again in 1914. And at that time 179 more Buddha images, seated, standing, and walking, and made of silver, crystal, and bronze, were found inside the stupa.

The Pra Bang image was housed at Wat Wisun from the time of its removal from Wat Manolom in 1513 until 1707, and once again, following its two-century sojourn in Vientiane and Bangkok, from 1867 until 1887.

Wat Aham. Adjacent to the Wat Wisun compound, and connected to it by a large gateway, are the precincts of Wat Aham (see Colour Plate 5), where, prior to the founding of the monastery, the

30

city's major tutelary shrine, dedicated to the *devata luang*, Pu No and Na No, was located. The monastery's *sim*, like its neighbouring Wat Wisun, was built by King Photthisarat, renowned as one of Luang Prabang's most devout Buddhist rulers. In 1527, to the dismay of his subjects, the king went so far as to ban the worship of *phi*, the *devata luang* shrine was demolished, and a Buddhist temple was built in its place. The expulsion was not final, however: the shrine was the most important spirit shrine in the city, and following its destruction, catastrophes including pestilence and bad weather that hindered the growth of the crops befell Luang Prabang. The people attributed the calamities to the expulsion of the *devata luang*, and after the king moved his court to Vientiane (in 1563), the shrine was eventually rebuilt (Le Boulanger, 1934, pp. 72–3). It still existed alongside the Buddhist temple in the mid-twentieth century, and although it no longer survives, Pu No and Na No are said to reside in two large banyan trees growing in the Wat Aham monastery grounds.

For many centuries Wat Aham was the residence of the head of Luang Prabang's Buddhist monkhood as well as the *devata luang*. The present *sim* dates from 1818.

Wat Sieng Thong. Wat Sieng Thong (Colour Plates 11–15), according to Luang Prabang's legendary history, occupies the site at the confluence of the Mekong and the Nam Khan where (the legend reports) the two hermits founded Luang Prabang by laying the city's first boundary stone. A different legend contends that it was here also that a humble merchant of betel named Chanthapanit fulfilled the hermits' prophecy by building a royal palace on the spot and becoming Sieng Dong-Sieng Thong's first king. Chanthapanit is also credited with the founding of Wat Sieng Thong. A mosaic on the rear of the monastery's *sim* (Colour Plate 16) depicts a 'tree of life' thought to commemorate the magnificent flame-of-the-forest tree believed to have once grown nearby.

More historically reliable records state that Wat Sieng Thong was constructed by King Setthathirat in 1560 on a site thought to be occupied by two *naga* who resided at the confluence of the Mekong and the Nam Khan; and two shrines dedicated to the

31

naga were preserved at Wat Sieng Thong until recent times. The monastery also played an important royal role: a ceremonious stairway led from the Mekong to the entrance of the monastery, and it was there that important visitors entered the city before being presented to the king. The king himself arrived via the stairway when he visited the monastery on ceremonial days to perform his religious duties.

Wat Sieng Thong's large *sim* (see Plate 8; Colour Plate 11) is the best example of the northern Lao classic style of architecture the city has to offer. Its high peaked roof with overlapping layers of glazed tile sweeps close to the ground; a large *dok so fa*, symbol of the universe, surmounts the top level.

Wat Tat Chom Si. Tat Chom Si (see Plates 1, 19, and 20; Colour Plate 1) is located at the summit of the sacred hill, Phu Si, and is reached by a stairway of 350 steps. Like Wat Sieng Thong, Tat Chom Si is said to have been built by the legendary king, Chanthapanit, and according to some, like Tat Luang, is said to contain a Buddhist relic. Its real ritual significance, however, depends on other legends, which tell of the defeat of some of Luang Prabang's oldest enemies: a powerful *naga* who guarded his earthly treasures of golden nuggets from a pit at the bottom of Phu Si; and unruly villagers who tried to steal the *naga's* vast treasure for themselves. After both the *naga* and the greedy villagers were vanquished, the golden nuggets were said to have been used to build the Chom Si stupa, and the nasty villagers were ordered to continuously strike cymbals, gongs, and drums to keep away the evil *naga* forever. Until the mid-twentieth century, cymbals were housed near the stupa, and during ceremonial events, the aboriginal Kha, whose land the Lao had invaded, were charged with clanging them repeatedly to banish whatever evil spirits might be present.

Historically, the Chom Si stupa is known to have been enlarged in 1796, and the stupa one sees there in the late twentieth century is even newer. It can be suggested, however, that the stupa's base story, sculpted in the form of a step pyramid from Phu Si's rocky summit (Colour Plate 17), was, prior to the building of any *tat*, a

32

shrine dedicated to spirits of the earth rather than relics of the Buddha.

Wat Mai (The New Monastery). One of the largest and most visually impressive of Luang Prabang's monasteries, Wat Mai (see Plate 7 and Colour Plates 2–4) is situated just north of the royal palace at the foot of Phu Si and is said to have been built in 1796. Wat Mai is the city's 'royal monastery' and is known especially as the home of the Pra Bang after Wat Wisun was destroyed in 1887. In the first half of the twentieth century it was the centre of some of the city's most important ceremonies.

Much more will be said about Wat Mai and its rituals in the following chapters.

4

The Royal City: Rites and Festivals

WHILE Luang Prabang's topographical layout—the position of its hills and rivers, its shrines and temples—defined the city spatially, its rituals and festivals conceptualized the city and the kingdom in temporal terms. At Luang Prabang (as in some other areas of South-East Asia such as Siam and Cambodia), one major festival was held each lunar month, thereby structuring the yearly calendar, defining the seasons, and marking the planting cycles by means of which agricultural peoples organize their lives. The monthly festivals, geared thus to the phases of the moon and the changing of the seasons, have been characterized as the 'downbeats and fulcrums around which the rest of the year was organized' (Zago, 1972, p. 284 n. 8).

If Luang Prabang was never the most ancient or the largest or the most famous of the world's capitals, it was without doubt one of the most complexly ceremonial. In fact, each of its monthly festivals comprised a collection of rites and ceremonies that reduplicated gestures and utterances that had been handed down, generation to generation, from the pre-historic, legendary past. Thus, the rituals brought to life many layers of mythological, religious, and political thought that collectively made up the Laotian world order. The guardian protectors of Luang Prabang and its territories, the *devata luang*, Pu No and Na No, who had hacked a way through the primeval forest and vanquished its unwelcoming inhabitants in order to found the city, were prominently represented, as were the Kha, whose land the invading Lao had vanquished. Playing a pivotal role in the ceremonies was Luang Prabang's king, who, as direct descendant of the mythological founders of the old Muang Sawa and the kingdom of Lan Sang, protected the lands politically as well as territorially.

With the adoption of Theravada Buddhism and the construction of *wat,* yet another layer of symbolic meaning was added to the old ceremonies. The new religion had its own annual cycle of holy days, and many of its traditions were grafted onto the old agricultural and territorial ones. The city's most important *wat*—Sawankhalok, Tat Luang, Wisun, Aham, Sieng Thong, and Mai—became the sites of rituals in which Buddhist, pre-Buddhist, and royal traditions met, overlapped, and meshed. Many of the rites centred around the Pra Bang image, palladium of the kingdom, thereby uniting the royal and religious realms.

Two of Luang Prabang's monthly festivals were exceptionally complex in amalgamating the city's and the kingdom's multiple cultural strains: the Twelfth Month Festival, or the Festival of the Tat, which took place in October and November; and the Fifth Month Festival, which was also the Festival of the New Year, in April and May.

The Festival of the Twelfth Month

Of all Luang Prabang's monthly festivals, the Twelfth Month Festival focused on traditions that perhaps reached furthest back into the remote, legendary past. Held for an entire month beginning with the full moon in October, the festival appears to have been in its earliest stage an agricultural rite associated with the cult of the soil, the latter thought to have been the popular religion of peoples throughout mainland South-East Asia and southern China long before Buddhist practices were adopted. October marked the end of Luang Prabang's rainy season and the end of the planting cycle on which the Lao depended for the cultivation of their rice crops. The rites of the Twelfth Month invoked the deities of the soil and the water to renew for another year the agricultural cycle on which the welfare of the people and the prosperity of the kingdom depended (Archaimbault, 1972, pp. 11–120; 1973, pp. 20–62, and *passim*).

On the thirteenth day of the new moon of the twelfth month, Luang Prabang's royal boatmen, dressed in red jackets and red hats bordered with yellow, removed the royal barges from a shed behind the king's palace and slid them down the steep banks of the Mekong to the embarcadero (Plates 14 and 15). From there the boatmen

14. Ceremonial boat lowered down the banks of the Mekong; above, buildings in the royal palace compound. (From a woodblock print by Louis Delaporte, in Garnier, 1873, Vol. 1)

proceeded towards the northern tip of the city where the Mekong and the Nam Khan meet. It was there that the city's founders, the two ascetics described in Chapter 3, had placed a stone that prophesied the foundation of the city and where the fifteen *naga* deities had been invoked to protect it. The confluence of the two rivers was also the site of many rocks that were favourite resting places for the guardian *naga* who ploughed their way up and down the waterways.

When, during the Twelfth Month Festival, the boatmen reached the confluence, they drew up to the sacred rocks and placed two floral arrangements on each. A candle the length of the king's forearm was placed in each bouquet, and, lighting the candles, the boatmen, as in the legendary past, beseeched the *naga* to protect the country and its people during the coming year. Then the boats

15. Indigenous drawing of ceremonial boat and oarsmen. (From Pavie et al., Vol. 5)

retraced their journey and, arriving at the southern boundary of the city, made offerings on the rock at the mouth of the Huei Hop, where the *naga* had asked the Buddha to leave his footprint.

An essential duty of the *naga* was to assure the annual flooding and drainage of the rice-fields, on which the cultivation of the rice crop depended. At the beginning of the dry season, when the small streams and ponds in the rice-fields were beginning to dry, the serpents had to leave their wet-season abodes to inhabit the large rivers that surrounded the city. To ensure the *naga*'s annual migration to the rivers and the drying of the rice-fields, Luang Prabang's boatmen in their ceremonial skiffs descended the rapids of the Mekong with their paddles raised horizontally so that the boats were propelled through the waters by the river itself. Thereby, it was thought, the course was opened up for the migration of the *naga* so that their former abodes would dry and the rice could be harvested. During the Ninth Month Festival of the following year, the rites would be repeated so that the *naga* would return to the ponds and streams and a new rice crop could be planted.

There is no way to know how long the regatta was practised as the major rite of the Twelfth Month, but with the founding of the Lan Sang Kingdom and the adoption of Buddhism, the focus of the rituals changed. The concept of yearly renewal was extended to include political matters as well as agricultural. In order for the kingdom to survive and prosper, the legitimacy of the king and his chieftains and the loyalty of their subjects had to be re-established, and eventually royal rites enacted on the esplanade of the royal stupa took centre-stage. Of all Luang Prabang's monthly festivals, the Festival of the Tat was the most important in terms of royal participation and the unification of the kingdom's diverse cultural, ethnic, and religious facets. At the Festival of the Tat, the king received oaths of allegiance from the chieftains of all his territories, thereby ensuring their loyalty for another year.

The main events of the Festival of the Tat took place on the fifteenth day of the new moon of the Twelfth Month on the wide esplanade that faced Tat Luang, which, according to (historically unsupported) legend, had been founded by the Indian King Asoka (Chapter 3) in the third century BC. King Asoka is considered by Buddhists everywhere as the ultimate exemplification of the perfect Buddhist king, whom later Buddhist kings wished to emulate. At the culmination of the Twelfth Month ceremonies, the king of Lan Sang, seated on a high platform constructed for the occasion next to Tat Luang, the Si Dharma Asoka stupa, meditated for a full week, during which time he was believed to assimilate the essence of Asoka and the perfections of the Buddhist Law.

The entire community took part in the ceremonies. In his royal procession to the Tat, the king was accompanied by nine cortèges: the Buddhist monkhood attired in their saffron robes; masked and costumed dancers representing Pu No and Na No, accompanied by richly caparisoned elephants; officers of the king in their royal uniforms and insignia; the children of the king, pulled in a coach; dignitaries from the surrounding *muang*; the guards and servants of the palace, who proceeded two by two on horseback; the royal musicians and bearers of ceremonial objects; the queens and their retinue; and, finally, the royal cooks and tailors. Not included in the procession itself but conspicuous none the less were the Kha,

1. Tat Chom Si. (Betty Gosling)

2. Gilt relief on the *sim* at Wat Mai showing deities seated in a Laotian landscape. (Betty Gosling)

3. Depiction of *devata* surrounded by a vegetal décor. Entrance to the *sim* at Wat Mai. (Betty Gosling)

4. Monastery compound (Wat Mai) as seen from Phu Si. (Betty Gosling)

5. *Sim* and stupas at Wat Aham. (Betty Gosling)

6. Chapel at Wat Sieng Thong. (Betty Gosling)

7. Stupa, chapel, and roof of the *sim* at Wat Sieng Thong. (Betty Gosling)

8. Tat Luang. (Betty Gosling)

9. Si Mahatat. (Betty Gosling)

10. Tat Makmo. (Betty Gosling)

11. *Sim* at Wat Sieng Thong. (Betty Gosling)

12. Chapel at Wat Sieng Thong. (Betty Gosling)

13. Chapel at Wat Sieng Thong. (Betty Gosling)

14. Entrance to the *sim* at Wat Sieng Thong. (Betty Gosling)

15. Decor on external wall of the *sim* at Wat Sieng Thong. (Betty Gosling)

16. Mosaic depiction of the 'Tree of Life' on the *sim* at Wat Sieng Thong. (Betty Gosling)

17. Pyramidal base of Tat Chom Si. (Betty Gosling)

18. A contemporary *wat*. (Betty Gosling)

19. House built of traditional materials: bamboo and wood. (Betty Gosling)

20. Traditional house with lower storey enclosed in stucco siding. (Betty Gosling)

21. Shop-house. (Betty Gosling)

22. French colonial mansion, now the Hotel Villa de la Princesse. (Betty Gosling)

the original inhabitants of the land, whom the Lao had vanquished in order to found their city, and who now cleared the processional way by incessantly rattling bamboo clappers.

On the esplanade, where all the townspeople had gathered, there was fun and laughter and merrymaking. In spite of the solemnity of the occasion everyone was allowed to laugh and sing and, as in other of Luang Prabang's festivals, a carnival atmosphere surrounded the sacred. Clad in great shaggy coats constructed from long strands of raffia and monstrous red masks with huge white eyes, giant teeth, and crinkled hair, the dancers representing Pu No and Na No danced their ritual dances (Plate 16). The dance was more than entertainment, for the movements of the *devata luang* re-enacted the founding of the Lan Sang Kingdom, the creation of the Laotian world, and the birth of the Lao people. In accordance with a legendary tradition quite separate from the dynastic legends, Pu No and Na No were not only the city's protectors, but its ancestors as well. With their ritual dance, the world was created, and the chaotic elements that had been dispelled when the Lao first made their way to Luang Prabang were banished once again for the coming year.

The most spectacular event of the Festival of the Tat was the launching of ceremonial wood and bamboo rockets (*bang fai*) from huge scaffolds that had been erected on the esplanade near the Tat. It was the *bang fai* that embodied most comprehensively the complexities of the Twelfth Month rituals. Not only did they provide entertainment for the fun-loving Lao people, but they also symbolized the temporal and the spatial framework of the kingdom: the transition of its seasons and the configuration of its territories. Ornamented with the heads of *naga* constructed of paper, the rockets commemorated the city's guardian serpents, the prime perpetuators of the temporal cycle. And the rockets themselves, ritually presented to the king by the saffron-robed monks from *wat* in the four quarters of the city—Wat Wisun (see Plate 10), Wat Sawankhalok, Wat Mai (see Plate 7), and Wat Sieng Thong (see Colour Plate 11)—exemplified the four quarters of the kingdom. In another of Luang Prabang's royal ceremonies, the king visited the directional *wat* to pay his respects to the monks and the

16. Dancers portraying the *devata luang*, Pu No and Na No. (From
   Archaimbault, 1972. Photograph Coutard)

Buddha images. On the full moon of the Twelfth Month, however,
the Laotian world converged on the royal stupa and the king.
Symbolically, Tat Luang was the centre of the Lao Kingdom.

Only when all these preliminaries had taken place did the king
receive the crucial oaths of allegiance from his subjects. Once more
the Kha had been conquered; the prosperity of the crops on which

the welfare of the people depended had been assured; the legitimacy of the king was renewed. The mythic and historic past merged with the present, the monarch ruled eternally, and with the rites completed, Luang Prabang was ready for another ceremonially structured year.

The Festival of the Fifth Month

While Luang Prabang's Twelfth Month Festival centred on Tat Luang, the Festival of the New Year, which took place in the Fifth Month, centred around Luang Prabang's palladium image, the Pra Bang. Although the Laotian New Year began in December, the Fifth Month (April) marked the initiation of the agricultural year that had been promised by the rites of the Twelfth. In April the days lengthened and the first life-bestowing rains foretold the season when trees and flowers would spring to life. Thus, the Fifth Month was a time for rejoicing, for dressing in one's best and most colourful clothes, and for visiting friends and relatives. More than any other monthly festival, the one held at the New Year was notable for the gaiety, fun, and exhilaration, in the midst of which the more serious and solemn rituals were enacted (Pavie et al., Vol. 7, pp. 228–30; Deydier, 1954, pp. 113–97; LeBar and Suddard, 1960, pp. 56–7; Archaimbault, 1973, p. 19).

But even the most popular and seemingly frivolous events followed certain time-honoured traditions whereby all of Luang Prabang's inhabitants—young and old, common and royal, animal and human—became participants in the ritual perpetuation of the life and structure of the kingdom. In April, Luang Prabang, usually languid and peaceful, sprang to life, and for three weeks ceremonies, rituals, and games succeeded one another almost without interruption. The sound of gongs, bells, drums, and tambourines deafened one's ears, while the entire city paraded through streets newly adorned with streamers of coloured paper bearing the signs of the zodiac. Dozens of the king's royal elephants were paraded by the aboriginal Kha, dressed in their red and yellow uniforms and helmet-like hats; and, surrounded by portable altars, banners, and guards, processions of colourful, ornately carved palanquins bore

41

the royal and Buddhist dignitaries. Small *tat*, made of sand, were constructed in the temple courtyards and along the river-banks, and near the palace a large and festive market transformed the area into a virtual fairground. This was no ordinary market, for there was nothing dead, no fish or meat to be cooked and eaten. Instead, at this special market there were only live animals—turtles, lizards, mice, squirrels, frogs, fish, and birds—which the people bought in cages and then, as acts of merit, liberated into the burgeoning, euphoric world.

But the world also had to be purified for the coming year. In each house women swept the floors and ceilings in order to expel any unfriendly spirits that may have come to live there. Laughing and shouting, the young people ran in bands through the streets, the boys brandishing stalks of greenery, symbols of growth and re-newal, while the girls, with flowers in their hair and golden sashes across their chests, carried buckets of water to pour on the young men. With much hilarity, the girls chased the crowds of boys through the lanes and streets, and no one was allowed to escape. In the ambience of fun and merriment that the New Year symbol-ized, the boys accepted their showering with good humour and more laughter.

Although, apparently, the dousing was initially intended as a rite of purification, the water was more often than not dark and muddy: the rites were friendly games of combat more than acts of cleansing. Such were the fun and games that, according to a de-scription of the festivities in 1887, the girls threw not only water, but taunted the boys by smearing them with mud, fish water, vari-ous kinds of oil, and lampblack. And, according to that same description, the victims included not only the fun-loving youths, but Buddhist monks and the princes and nobles who made their way in elaborate procession along the main streets. Apparently, the tradition was well established, for the princes, usually elaborately at-tired in ceremonial garb, on this occasion dressed with a minimum of clothing so that their royal costumes would not be soiled!

The core of the Fifth Month Festival was not the soaking of people, however, but the ceremonial aspersion of the Buddha im-ages in the major *wat*, a true and respected gesture of cleansing and renewal, such as the new year's rains would bring. For the aspersion of the Pra Bang in 1887, the king, escorted in a procession of royal elephants, nobility, and princes (scantily dressed), assembled on the courtyard of Wat Wisun, the site of the legendary rice-fields of the kingdom's protectors, Pu No and Na No, and, in April of 1887, the abode of the Pra Bang.

Although the main purpose of the ceremonies appears to have been the aspersion of the palladium image, the land on which it was located had to be purified first. While the royal officials were changing into their princely robes, preparations were also being made for Pu No and Na No to perform their cleansing dance. Adjoining Wat Wisun, at Wat Aham (see Colour Plate 5) was the Pu No–Na No tutelary shrine and a small bamboo shed where, between ceremonies, the Pu No and Na No ritual masks and costumes were stored. After offerings of candles, bananas, and bowls of rice were made, the clothing was ceremonially removed and donned by the dancers who would impersonate the kingdom's protectors. To the beat of drums and the laughter and chatter of the people, Pu No and Na No danced on their former rice-fields in order to dispel the evil spirits that might still be inhabiting them. The Pu No and Na No dancers concluded their performance by paying respect to the king on behalf of all Lao peoples, past, present, and future.

After the destruction of Wat Wisun in 1887, not long after the Festival of the Fifth Month described above had ended, the Pra Bang image was, until the mid-twentieth century, housed in Wat Mai, the royal *wat*, situated next to the king's palace, and the ceremonies continued to be culminated there even after the image was removed, once again, to the royal palace. As described in 1953, the Pra Bang was removed by the monks from its customary altar inside the palace and placed in a *prasat*, a small carved wooden palace-like structure, which was carried on the shoulders of ceremonially costumed Kha to the accompaniment of their tambourines and placed in the middle of the Wat Mai courtyard. Aspersion of the image was performed by means of a *hanglin*, a long bamboo or wooden pole carved in the shape of a *naga* (see Plate 6). Lustral water was poured into the tail of the *naga*, and from there it flowed through a narrow

17. One of the *devata luang*, Pu No and Na No, aspersing the Pra Bang through a *hanglin*. (From Renaud, 1930)

trough to its head, where it emerged through the serpent's mouth onto the head of the image placed beneath it. Aspersion was ritually performed by all the people: the monks, the nobles, the king, and the Pu No and Na No dancers (Plate 17), who, like the guardian *naga* spirit who conveyed the water, played their roles in preserving the socio-political and religious structure in which Luang Prabang's existence for over half a millennium was so deeply ingrained (Deydier, 1954, pp. 155–7).

In the late nineteenth century, Luang Prabang's time-honoured, tightly structured mytho-historical world would be penetrated for the first time by Europeans, the French, who would rule over Luang Prabang for the next sixty years. But even then the ritual life of the city and all its multi-layered rituals persisted. Disruption would come, not with the arrival of the Europeans, but from some of Luang Prabang's closest neighbours, the Vietnamese, in the second half of the twentieth century.

For those happenings, it is necessary to consider Luang Prabang as viewed from the outside—as experienced by the foreigners who came to love, to protect, or to vanquish the birthplace and ceremonial pivot of the Laotian world.

5

Luang Prabang and the Outside World: Arrival of the French

IN spite of the Laotian concept of Luang Prabang as the centre of the Laotian world, and despite its involvement in the political affairs of mainland South-East Asia, at mid-nineteenth century the Indo-Chinese peninsula had yet to be fully explored, and the old royal city had not received a single European visitor. When French travellers began to arrive at Luang Prabang, in 1861, Laos had been under Siamese rule for nearly a century, and during that time there had been infrequent mention of Luang Prabang in the Siamese chronicles (Flood and Flood, 1978, pp. 175–6). Mgr. Jean-Baptiste Pallegoix, bishop of a Catholic mission in Bangkok, in his 1854 history of Siam, listed Luang Prabang among the country's eighteen tributary states, and in a brief sketch of the province, based on Siamese reports, he noted that since the destruction of Vientiane, in 1828, Luang Prabang had greatly expanded and had a lively trade with the Lolo people of southern China (Pallegoix, 1854, p. 49). Information among other Europeans was equally vague and some-times contradictory. While there were rumours that the city was inhabited by descendants of ancient Laotian kings, others con-sidered it to be 'the modern capital of Laos', founded recently, after the fall of Vientiane (*The French in Indo-China*, 1884, p. 78).

Although there appears to have been little at the royal city to attract non-Asian visitors, the European world was intrigued by the territories that surrounded it. As one European wrote in 1884:

Speculation was rife concerning the secrets hid in those vast forests and intricate maze of mountains and river gorges, but until within the last twenty years, science has had little definite knowledge to impart. The sources and the courses of the mighty streams; the trend and elevation of the dividing ranges; the political divisions and the still more complex boundary-lines of the different races, languages, and religions; the customs and the stage of civilization of the various tribes; the luxuriant and wonderful plant and animal life of the interior—these were among the matters about which the West was strongly and vainly excited (*The French in Indo-China*, 1884, pp. 9–10).

At the centre of this unexplored area was Luang Prabang, which would, because of its location and agreeable setting, prove to be the major halting place of many explorers during their probes into the surrounding rivers and forests.

Unfortunately, the inhabitants of Luang Prabang left no accounts of the white men who came to investigate their lands, and we can view the intrusions only through foreign eyes. But those observations are enlightening. In spite of the Europeans' lack of prior knowledge concerning the area (or perhaps because of it), their memoirs, unencumbered by historical fact, are fresh and lively and filled with serendipitous delight. While Luang Prabang's architecture and rituals show how the city functioned as a royal capital, the European accounts, paradoxically, help to explain how the city (in spite of foreign intervention) has been able to retain the comparative isolation that allowed the old traditions to persist.

The first European to visit Luang Prabang was the French naturalist-explorer, Henri Mouhot, employed by the English and better known for his 'discovery', in 1860, of Angkor Wat, in Cambodia. Mouhot was not the first European to visit Angkor, but he was the first to fully appreciate the architectural wonders of the old Khmer city and to publicize them to the Western world. His acclaim is not undeserved. But Mouhot was first and foremost a naturalist, and, after his visit to Angkor and a brief return to his base city, Bangkok, he proceeded by bullock cart and elephant-back overland across the Khorat plateau (north-east Thailand) to northern Laos in search of botanical, zoological, and ethnographic materials. He arrived in Luang Prabang in July 1861.

According to Mouhot, Luang Prabang was:

a delightful little town, covering a square mile of ground and containing a population, not as Mgr. Pallegoix says in his work on Siam, of 80,000, but of 7,000 or 8,000 only. The situation is very pleasant. The mountains which, above and below this town, enclose the Mekong, form here a kind of circular valley or amphitheater, nine miles in diameter, and which, there can be no doubt, was anciently a lake.

The landmarks that Mouhot noted did not vary much from those that the Lao legends had singled out as determining factors in the founding of the city. Although, as Mouhot noted, the town was located on both sides of the Mekong, the major, central portion was situated between the two rivers that surrounded the isolated mount, Phu Si, which he estimated to be more than 100 metres high. The hill was surmounted by a stupa that later visitors would identify as Tat Chom Si.

Mouhot described the city and its surroundings in idyllic (and Eurocentric) terms: the rivers reminded him of the beautiful lakes of Como and Geneva. And 'were it not for the constant blaze of a tropical sun, or if the mid-day heat were tempered by a gentle breeze, the place would be a little paradise'. He was also enchanted by the Nam Khan: 'The moon shines with extraordinary brilliancy, silvering the surface of this lovely river, bordered by high mountains, looking like a grand and gloomy rampart. The chirp of the crickets alone breaks the stillness. In my little cottage all is calm and tranquil; the view from my window is charming.'

While Mouhot's impressions of Luang Prabang were ones of delight, the reaction of the Lao to the 'long-bearded stranger', as he was referred to, were somewhat different. According to Mouhot's account, nothing could have caused such a sensation as his arrival.

From the humblest to the greatest—for even here are distinctions of rank—everyone looks on a 'white' as a natural curiosity, and they are not yet satisfied with looking—nothing is talked of but the stranger. When I pass through the town in my white dress, to go to the market or to visit the pagodas [*sim*] or other interesting places, the people crowd round me, and look after me as long as they can catch a glimpse of me.

The local people were friendly and helpful, however, and Mouhot wrote: 'Luckily it is not here as in Siam; the natives are willing to help me, and for a few inches of brass wire I get a beautiful longicorn or some other insect, and these are brought to me on all sides: thus I have succeeded in largely increasing my [entomological] collection.'

The Lao king, Tiantha, agreed to receive the stranger, and, as reported by Mouhot:

After waiting for ten days I have at length been presented to the king with great pomp. The reception room was a shed such as they build in our villages on fête-days, but larger and hung with every possible color. His Majesty was enthroned at one end of the hall, lazily reclining on a divan, having on his right hand four guards squatting down, and each holding a saber; behind were the princes all prostrated, and farther off the senators, with their backs to the public and their faces in the dust.

Having been officially received, Mouhot made several trips out of Luang Prabang during the following months, and he described the peoples, flora, and fauna of Luang Prabang's surrounding territories and reported the killing of a tiger. But his exploration of the lands around Luang Prabang was not to continue. During his last journey away from the capital, Mouhot was attacked by fever and three weeks later, on 10 November 1861, he died, just a few hours from his 'little paradise'. Fittingly, he was buried near the banks of the Nam Khan, about which he had written so rhapsodically (Mouhot, 1864, pp. 137, 141, 143–61, 268–9, and 272–3).

More important to most nineteenth-century Europeans than the observation of the beauties and scientific wonders of nature was the search for a trade route 'through those wild countries to the fabulously wealthy regions of Western China' (*The French in Indo-China*, 1884, p. 10). By the mid-nineteenth century, French explorers had settled at the mouth of the Mekong; Saigon (now Ho Chi Minh City) had been captured in 1861; and Cambodia had been placed under French protection in 1863. Similarly, Great Britain was making headway with the exploration and control of the Irrawaddy and Chao Phraya rivers in Burma and Siam. Eager to make their own claim to the fortunes of Asia's vast interiors and the great wealth they thought lay waiting for them in China, the French planned to follow the course of the Mekong, possibly to its source, which they speculated (correctly) to be in Tibet, some 4500 kilometres from their point of departure, the mouth of the river, near Saigon. On their journeys to the interior of Asia, the explorers passed through, and often sojourned in, Luang Prabang.

In 1866, five years after Mouhot's journey to Luang Prabang, a party led by Doudart de Lagrée, a captain in the French navy, set out from Saigon, not by land, as Mouhot had travelled, but by boat along the Mekong. Lagrée was a staunch colonialist who launched his expedition in the hopes of opening up the last unexplored areas of Asia for French exploitation, to make friends with and elicit commitments from local authorities, to publicize and celebrate the French, and to find a suitable trade route for the transportation of goods from and into China.

Through what regions did the Mekong flow? Who were the peoples who had access to it? Was its source really in Tibet, or perhaps, as some claimed, a huge lake in upper Laos? These were things the explorers did not know, and the published goal of the expedition was to find the answers. Lagrée had only vague and contradictory information furnished by local peoples and some fragmentary and out-of-date European reports that dealt with the river a short distance from its mouth. There was much to be learned.

In the Lagrée party was its second-in-command, Francis Garnier, who documented the events of the inland journey, and the youngest of the group, Louis Delaporte, an artist who recorded the journey pictorially (and some of whose woodblock prints are reproduced here). According to Garnier's report, the Mekong was not a friendly river: the journey was encumbered by formidable rapids, more like waterfalls than cataracts; huge blocks and boulders of sandstone impeded travel and proved a constant danger; and heavy rains and flash-floods capsized their boats (Plate 18). Another member of the party, Louis de Carné, wrote of the river which 'loses itself in a labyrinth of islets, of weeds, and of trees arising from the bosom of the waters' (*The French in Indo-China*, 1884, p. 213). The thousands of channels formed an inextricable labyrinth that led only to unnavigable shallows.

But if Lagrée and his associates found the Mekong inhospitable, such was not the case with Luang Prabang, which the party reached in April 1867. The city was 1200 kilometres (direct) from their starting point, in Saigon, and the journey had taken over nine

18. Rapids on the Mekong south of Luang Prabang. (From a woodblock print by Louis Delaporte, in Garnier, 1873, Vol. 1)

months. One can picture the joy with which the party arrived. As described by Garnier, 'At eleven o'clock we turned the last bend that formed the river below Luang Prabang.... The city then appeared to us on the opposite bank, two miles distant. The glimpse that was offered us was most picturesque and lively.' Like Mouhot, Garnier noted the central mount, which 'rose like a dome of greenery' in the midst of grey thatched houses, and at the summit of the hill, the stupa with its pointed spire, which 'erupted from the foliage and formed the focal point of the land-scape (Plate 19). Several pagodas [sim] rose in tiers on the sides of this sacred mount, and their red roofs contrasted vividly with the deep green of the vegetation.'

At the foot of the hill, Garnier noted the king's palace, 'an enormous conglomeration of huts, surrounded by sturdy, high fences and forming a rectangle'. A stairway of several hundred steps, cut into the rock, led up the precipice directly to the 'sacred

19. The sacred hill, Phu Si. (From Pavie et al., Vol. 7)

pyramid' that crowned the summit, and around the base of the mount and along the river-banks, a large number of houses surrounded by high fences were aligned in parallel rows. Garnier described the streets bordered by the fences as large and very regular, crossing at right angles. Moreover,

at the foot of the river banks, 15 metres high, motionless rafts on which a number of huts were constructed, make up, below the city, a second one,

20. The Mekong with racks for drying fish (*centre front*) and on the far bank of the river, paths like boot laces. Above, centre: Phu Si and Tat Chom Si. (From a woodblock print by Louis Delaporte, in Garnier, 1873, Vol. 2)

with numerous footpaths, which appear from a distance as so many white boot laces that connect with the houses on the river bank.... On the opposite bank of the river are long rows of bamboo designed for drying fish [Plate 20]; a little beyond, gardens, some sparsely settled houses and pagodas and a range of hills, steep and denuded.... The banks across the Nam Kham display for a great distance in the interior an uninterrupted succession of pagodas, of large gardens in which betel vines grow and in which our botanist found for the first time peach trees, plum trees, and oleanders. We have entered a more temperate zone.

Luang Prabang's inhabitants proved no less hospitable than the environment. The local curiosity about Europeans had abated considerably since Mouhot's visit, and the people accepted the foreigners with little commotion. The French were soon able to explore the city without serious problems. Lagrée established an observation station on top of one of the city's tallest stupas; the party's geologist began searching the land and rivers for minerals and precious stones (without success); the botanist collected a rich harvest of new plant life; and Delaporte tripped from temple to temple avidly sketching the architecture. The local residents, who assumed that the party had arrived with the same intentions as Mouhot, inundated the dismayed botanist with insects.

On a more sombre note, Luang Prabang's king, Tiantha, upon Lagrée's request, supplied a stone to be carved and erected as a monument at Mouhot's gravesite. For Garnier the memorializing was a touching event: 'The landscape that framed the tomb is graceful and sad at the same time. Trees with dark green foliage shelter [the grave], and the murmur of their leaves mingles with the rumbling of the waters of the Nam Khan, which flows at their feet.'

But, while Garnier's account of his stay in Luang Prabang at times reflected Mouhot's idyllic descriptions, he was more interested in the town's wealth and bustling commercial life. Whereas Mouhot had described Luang Prabang as a 'pleasant little town', Garnier wrote that since his departure from Cochin-China he had not encountered such an agglomeration of houses. Garnier reported the number of households as approximately 16,000, double Mouhot's estimate. Moreover, hundreds of boats of all sizes plow their way up and down along the floating suburb along the banks of the river while large, heavy rafts coming down the river slowly search along the bank for a suitable place to dock and to discharge their merchandise [Plate 21]. Throngs of boatmen and porters move to the foot of the river bank, and there escapes a confused clamor that mingles with the murmurs of the river and the whisper of the palm trees that the wind rocks gently along the bank.... An extremely animated daily market is held under some sheds situated near the junction of the Nam Khan and the Mekong [Plate 22]; but they are insufficient to accommodate all the vendors, and open booths, stalls, or shops are prolonged for upwards of half a mile in a wide street parallel to the river. This was the first time since our departure from Phnom Penh that we have found a market in the European sense of the word.

Garnier pondered this sudden eruption of lively and thriving commercial life compared to other areas his party had passed through and suggested several explanations. In part he attributed it to the number of racial types that populated the city, and which he described as representing 'all the nations of Indo-China and India' (see Plate 3). He also attributed the rich commercial life to 'a radical difference in [Luang Prabang's] political regime'. He surmised that the more southerly regions of Laos had once been known for their wealth and commercial enterprise but that Siamese rule had

21. Boats on the banks of the Mekong at Luang Prabang. (From Pavie et al., Vol. 2)

55

22. Market scene at Luang Prabang. (From Pavie et al., Vol. 7)

ended their prosperity. Luang Prabang, in contrast, was relatively
free of Siamese domination, for it had the protection of Vietnam and
China, to whom it sent elephants as tribute. Luang Prabang was,
Garnier concluded, 'the most eminent Laotian center in Indo-
China, the place of refuge, the natural halting place of all the
peoples of the interior who want to escape the despotism of the
Siamese'.

One of the aims of the Lagrée mission was to persuade the king
of Luang Prabang that, despite his relative independence, Siamese

despotism was inevitable and that, while Asian domination was not tolerable, European colonization could be his salvation. As Garnier wrote: 'The suzerainty of an Asian government always signifies monopoly, obligatory transactions, and consequently, stagnation; European intervention in the nineteenth century ought to signify commercial freedom, progress, and wealth.' Thus, France could not abdicate its 'moral obligation' to direct and protect the movement of Indo-Chinese emancipation.

Needless to say, after Lagrée had sought and received an audience with the king and presented his opinions, relations between the Frenchmen and their hosts quickly deteriorated. According to Garnier, Lagrée's views were met with 'extreme coldness, marked by defiance and agitation'. The French scientific efforts to explore the Mekong appeared mysterious to the Laotian authorities and aroused their suspicions. Moreover, they were not impressed by Lagrée's claims that French domination would in no way threaten Luang Prabang's independence and that under French rule the Lao king's power could only increase. Matters seemed to improve somewhat as the weeks went by, however: Garnier made friends with a cousin of the king who supported the French views and converted the royal family. Apparently content with this turn of events, Lagrée and his party left the city to continue their exploration and exploitation northward toward China (see Garnier, 1873, pp. 316–28; Osborne, 1969).

Despite the rapport that the French appeared to have reached with Luang Prabang's royalty, however, ousting the Siamese was another matter altogether. It would be another quarter century before the Siamese relinquished their suzerainty over Luang Prabang and the French achieved their ultimate goal of ruling Luang Prabang and its provinces. Not until 1886 did the Siamese sanction a French vice-consulate in Luang Prabang, and not until 1893 did France achieve complete control.

The major figure in the transfer of power from Siam to France was Auguste Pavie, who, in 1869, had come to Indo-China as a sergeant in the French army and, having developed a strong interest in the peoples and cultures of South-East Asia, extended his stay as a survey geographer for the French. Pavie had been inspired by

Mouhot's and Garnier's explorations, and his warm empathy with the people far exceeded that of either of his predecessors. In 1885, Siam agreed to his appointment as the first European vice-consul to Laos, and he arrived at the royal city in February 1887.

Pavie expressed his joy: 'I am in Luang Prabang!' he wrote, the scenery 'a wonder to the eyes'. The city and its rivers and mountains he considered 'incontestably the most beautiful spot in Laos' (Pavie et al., Vol. 6, pp. 19 and 30). The Siamese officials who resided in the city were, on the other hand, considerably less delighted with the Frenchmen's arrival. Pavie and his party were put under tight watch by the two officials, the governors of Sukhothai and Phitsanulok, to whom the jurisdiction of the city had been entrusted. Leery of French intervention, the Siamese officials did their best to isolate the new diplomats, and Pavie was not allowed an audience with the king for several weeks.

Pavie described the official reception in detail. Although Luang Prabang's King Oun Kham, at the age of 76, was in ill health and feeble, the ceremonies with which he received the French were royally appropriate. Pavie and his party were conducted to the palace by an escort of both Siamese and Lao officials on streets that had been newly swept. The processional road to the palace had been cleared of people who, none the less, gathered at their doorways and at the cross-streets to see the procession as it passed.

The king's audience hall was an apartment of several rooms, and a large armchair for the king was located near the centre of the hall, with chairs for the princes on its right, and one for Pavie, flanked by two Siamese officials on the left. Behind the king's armchair was a table covered with wooden and bronze images of the Buddha, gilded and dusty. In front of them on a pedestal rested the royal paraphernalia: the ceremonial sword, and the boxes and vases of the royal betel set. Near the king's chair a table was set with teacups and golden teapots. At the back of the hall, the golden throne was situated under an immense white parasol of many tiers (Plate 23), and many rugs from Yunnan, red or blue with white designs, covered the floor (Pavie et al., Vol. 1, pp. 302–4; Vol. 6, pp. 23–8).

In spite of Siamese resistance, Pavie was able to make closer contact with the Lao officials through the king's close friend and

23. King Oun Kham in his palace seated beneath the royal white tiered parasol. (From Boudet and Masson, 1931)

confidant, the head monk of Wat Mai (Plate 24), who introduced himself simply as 'Satou' (Abbot) and later acted as go-between, conveying messages from the king without Siamese approval. When proper housing was denied the new French ambassadors, the Satou allowed them to live at Wat Mai (Pavie et al., Vol. 1, pp. 228 and 254; Vol. 6, pp. 39–41; Vol. 7, p. 255).

One of Pavie's most persistent requests was that he be allowed to see the palm-leaf manuscripts that he had learned were stored in the Wat Mai library. He had already collected a number of old stone inscriptions from various monasteries, and had been told that the history of old Lan Sang was recorded further in the manuscripts.

When he was finally given access to the documents, with the help of the Satou and two Cambodians who were able to read the Khmer parts of the manuscripts, he eagerly began to translate them into French. From these efforts the outside world got its first glimpse of Laotian history—of the two holy men and the flame-tree, of Fa Ngum and his descendants, of the division of the kingdom between Luang Prabang and Vientiane. The origin of the Tai people at Muang Then that was recorded in the old Khun Borom legend supported Pavie's earlier guess that, judging from its geography and the distribution of its population, Lan Sang had been founded by a migration of Lao that had arrived at Luang Prabang via the Nam Ou (Pavie et al., Vol. 1, p. 213; Vol. 3, p. 167; Vol. 6, pp. 111 and 124–43).

More personal contact with King Oun Kham became possible when for three days in June 1887, Chinese raiders attacked and plundered the royal city. All of Luang Prabang, including several of its monasteries and the royal palace, was set afire and the people fled. In the midst of the chaos, the old king was somehow left abandoned in his palace, and it was Pavie's Khmer

24. The Abbot, or Satou, of Wat Mai. (From Pavie et al., Vol. 2)

assistant, Keo, who risked the flames to save his life. Pavie and his party helped the king escape the pillaging invaders and tended the ailing monarch on their retreat down the Mekong. Moreover, Pavie helped organize the settlement of refugees who had fled their burning villages, and he and the king became affectionate friends, a relationship that is reflected often in Pavie's voluminous writings (Pavie et al., Vol. 6, pp. 76–108). The Siamese, who had abandoned the city during the Chinese siege, none the less threatened the Lao with future, more intense occupation, and King Oun Kham, with the help of Wat Mai's Satou, turned more and more to Pavie for support.

In spite of the devastation, Luang Prabang appears to have begun a quick recovery, and in 1888, only a year after the sack of the city, the French counted 1,200 newly built houses; 10,000 inhabitants (in 1887, the number had been estimated at 15,000); 45 *sim*; and 500 monks (Pavie et al., Vol. 1, p. 209; Vol. 7, p. 228). With close ties between the French and Luang Prabang's officials firmly established, the Siamese, in 1893, at last relinquished control of its lands on the eastern side of the Mekong to the French, and in 1894, Pavie became Laos's first French governor-general. Luang Prabang was now divided into two parts, Siamese on the west bank of the Mekong and French on the east, but, in 1906, with a new Siamese-French treaty that agreed to less arbitrary boundaries, Luang Prabang became wholly French.

Pavie's love of Luang Prabang and his cordial acceptance by its people was shared by his fellow countrymen. When Pavie and his officials arrived at Luang Prabang after it had become French territory (Plate 25), they were greeted warmly. The assistant to the chief of the French Mission, Pierre Lefèvre-Pontalis described their entry into the city. He noted his great satisfaction when, descending the Mekong, he glimpsed the spires of the Chom Si stupa at the summit of Phu Si and the confluence of the river with the Nam Khan. Pavie noted with what contentment he was now, on his sixth visit, returning to Luang Prabang, where he dreamed of encountering the gratitude of his old friends, the King and Queen and the Satou of Wat Mai (Pavie et al., Vol. 2, p. 271). To honour the arrival of the Commission, the King had sent ceremonial boats, red and gold, with ornate prows and a crew of musicians dressed in multicolour garments. The party disembarked, not as in the old

25. Members of the Pavie Mission: in the centre, in white suit, Auguste
Pavie; on his right, the Mission's doctor. M. Massie: on his left,
Luang Prabang's first French Commissioner, M. Vacle; surrounded
by other French officials, Cambodian translators, and Lao and
Vietnamese servants. (From Pavie et al., Vol. 1)

days on the stairs that led up the banks of the Nam Kham to the
French consulate, but on the royal stairway that led from the
Mekong to the king's palace. That evening, after meeting with
friends, old and new, they celebrated their arrival at the old capital
of Lan Sang, 'at last French!'.

26. French consulate and home of the first French commissioner. (From Pavie et al., Vol. 7)

The French were careful to observe the old traditions. One of their first visits was to their old friend the Satou whom, on earlier visits, Lefèvre-Pontalis had loved to visit. As the royal monastery and the abode of the Pra Bang, Wat Mai also had political significance, and the French presented the abbot with a ceremonial piece of yellow silk—testimony of gratitude from the president of France for the services the priest had rendered his people in the past (Pavie et al., Vol. 5, pp. 73–4).

Compared with the flamboyant display of royal traditions by the Lao, life for the French (as it is described in the Pavie accounts) seemed decidedly homy. The Siamese, like the Lao, recognized the importance of symbolically establishing their territorial rights and had situated their offices next to Wat Aham, the legendary rice-fields of Luang Prabang's *devata luang*. But M. Vacle, the new French commissioner, resided in the newly finished building that had been designed to house the French consul when the city was still under Siamese rule (Plate 26). The house was located some distance from the river on the opposite side of Phu Si from the palace, but, as described by Lefèvre-Pontalis, it was 'a princely edifice in teak and pine' with a grand hall aired by punkah and filled with couches, armchairs, tables, and curios. The dining room was hung with blue and white fabrics woven by the Meo, and the table was always set with flowers. The meals were well served, and the cuisine was said to be 'marvelously successful' (Pavie et al., Vol. 5, pp. 79–80).

The French appeared happy with their new home and well prepared to stay. As one might imagine, there were many difficulties that lay ahead, but, as time would tell, the French would remain in their new land for half a century.

6

The Persistence of Traditions
and the Preservation of the Past

IN spite of late nineteenth-century efforts such as Lagrée's and Garnier's to open up South-East Asia and south-west China for the exploitation of precious minerals and other transportable riches, those objectives turned out to be unrealistic. The Mekong's torrential rapids, its lurking boulders and sandbanks, the infusing vegetation that had impeded the Lagrée expedition all proved untameable, and the once hoped-for riches of China simply did not exist. Extensive travel by river even within Indo-China was not a practicality. As late as the 1930s, Milton Osborne (1969, p. 219) noted that it still took longer to travel by river from Saigon to Luang Prabang than to travel from Saigon to Marseilles (in France).

As a buffer state that helped protect French Indo-China from the threats of Siamese and British expansion, however, Luang Prabang served its protectors well. The tightly structured, mythological, and ceremonial world that over the centuries had formed the core of Luang Prabang's political, religious, and popular life bolstered the country's effectiveness against outside intervention. By 1899, a French *résident supérieur* in Vientiane ruled Luang Prabang and all of what is present-day Laos. But Luang Prabang's royal traditions offered charisma that was a decided asset: while the royal houses of Laos's central and southern provinces were reduced to the roles of provincial governors, Luang Prabang's king found support for his role as a reigning monarch. As the only officially recognized king in all of Laos, Luang Prabang's royalty was perhaps, more than ever before, free from the conflicts and expansive dispositions of its competing neighbours.

The royal family remained very much in evidence. When the health of Pavie's friend, King Oun Kham, deteriorated in 1894, a year after French rule began, he was succeeded by his son Sakkalin (Plate 27). According to Pierre Lefèvre-Pontalis, now the assistant

27. Prince Sakkalin. (From Pavie et al.,
    Vol. 2)

to the chief of the French mission, the new king 'exercised his
authority in debonair fashion' yet 'also, perhaps, with a certain
skepticism excusable in a prince who for a number of years, had
suffered the intervention of the Siamese and who had seen French
domination begin with the partition of his country and its capital

into two broken pieces'. As for lesser royalty, Lefèvre-Pontalis wrote, 'During my first stay, in 1890, I saw the princes only on official occasions when their initiative was effaced at every turn by that of the Siamese functionaries by whom they were flanked. This time I was able to judge them better, for a day does not pass without one or another of them coming to find us.' In spite of their authority, which was primarily hereditary and had extended over vast territories, the princes under everyday circumstances were hardly distinguishable from ordinary people. 'On the other hand,' Lefèvre-Pontalis continued, 'on certain occasions such as public fêtes they relive a part of the solemn traditions transmitted by the ancient kings of Lan Sang. Then, dressed again in sumptuous golden costumes, they are carried on palanquins through the streets of the city, appearing everywhere only when adorned with a variety of royal insignia' (Pavie et al., Vol. 5, pp. 77–8).

All the pomp and ceremony did not mean, however, that the Lao did not respect the French in their role as official rulers of their kingdom. For the cremation of King Oun Kham in 1896, elaborate ceremonies were planned for the esplanade of Tat Luang, where royal cremations were traditionally held. This time, however, there was a problem, for according to Lao tradition, royal funeral pyres should be lit by a fire originating in the kingdom's capital city, which, of course, was now Paris. The French Commissioner, M. Vacle, was unable to arrange for a torch to be delivered all the way from Europe, but a more practical solution was devised. The Lao were well aware that the cables that had lately crossed their skies were in fact telegraph (*tac-tac*) wires that connected them with France. A generator was installed at Wat Tat Luang, and an electrical spark was transmitted to it via the telegraph wires from Paris. Much to the relief of the French Commissioner, the cremation pyre ignited, and the ritual requirements were maintained. Another layer of mythology had been added to the old, traditional rites (Raquez, 1902, p. 349).

* * *

In 1954, the end of French rule in Indo-China brought about traumatic political changes that would once again, as in the past, engender conflicts between Laos and its neighbours and among the Lao themselves. In 1945, shortly before the end of the Second World War, the Japanese had entered Luang Prabang and demanded that King Sisavang Vong declare its independence from France, and in 1947, the old kingdom of Lan Sang became a constitutional monarchy with a Western-style parliamentary government centred in Vientiane. The French had done nothing to prepare the country for independent rule, however, and its boundaries, arbitrarily drawn by the Siamese and the French in the late nineteenth and early twentieth centuries, did not take into account ethnic divisions that divided the land more deeply than boundary lines. War was inevitable.

In spite of the burgeoning turmoil, as late as the early 1950s, many of Luang Prabang's royal traditions were still intact. In the spring of 1953, the city was imminently threatened by Vietnamese forces that were invading Laos from the east—an event that the entire world was watching. Reporters from *France Soir*, *Figaro*, and *The New York Times* waited in Luang Prabang for news from the battlefields. There were more white men in the city than anyone could ever remember. But most of Luang Prabang was unconcerned. It was April; the joyful New Year's Festival of the Fifth Month was in progress; the king, the princes, the monks, and Pu No and Na No were preparing to asperse the Pra Bang. The Pra Bang would protect the city and its people from harm (Deydier, 1954, pp. 133–97).

Now, of course, there were also differences: the king, dressed in his ceremonial *sampot* and crown of gold, bore the Cross of the Legion of Honour as well as the Esteemed Ribbon of the Million Elephants (Plate 28). And the princes and nobles, who had once so conspicuously paraded the streets in their royal insignia, had been replaced by constitutionally appointed officials. While the Kha still carried the Pra Bang to Wat Mai for the culmination of the ceremonies, now they were escorted by the national army in white uniforms, rifles instead of sabres at their shoulders. At Wat Mai, where the Pra Bang was to be lustrated, the rites were performed

28. King Sisavang Vong in *sampot*, crown, and insignia.
(From Renaud, 1930)

not only by the king but by the country's prime minister and other important government dignitaries who had arrived from Vientiane for the ceremonies. As in the olden days, all of Luang Prabang crowded the streets while the dignitaries aspersed the Pra Bang positioned beneath the *hanglin*.

Amidst the festivities of the New Year and the persistent confidence that the Pra Bang would protect Luang Prabang from the invading Vietnamese, some of the city's more serious-minded officials urged King Sisavang Vong and his family to flee to safety in the southern part of Laos and to take the Pra Bang with them. But the king refused: the Pra Bang should not leave its capital; for five hundred years the Vietnamese had not managed to enter the royal city, and he himself would not leave until the Vietnamese forces were repulsed.

The city was not invaded, and Sisavang Vong continued to rule at Luang Prabang until his death, in 1959. Already, by the mid-1950s, however, the Pra Bang had forfeited its role as protector of the kingdom. When a coalition government that attempted to neutralize the nationalist and Vietnamese–Pathet Lao communist forces was formed, the Pra Bang, the ultimate symbol of the monarchy, conspicuously tipped the hoped-for balance of power in favour of the royally supported nationalists. The Pra Bang ceased to be the centre of ritual events, and, according to some sources, it was quietly whisked away to Vientiane, or, perhaps, even to Moscow. It would not be long before the Laotian monarchy would lose its potency as well.

On the death of Sisavang Vong, he was succeeded by his son, Sisavang Vatthana, and, some believe, the new king ruled from the new French palace for eighteen years, until Laos succumbed to communist Pathet Lao forces in 1975. In 1977, an insurgency in which the king was said to be involved brought about his demise: the former king and his family were banished to a location in northern Laos near the Vietnamese border, where, it was reported, they died in captivity. Official government documents tell a different story, however. According to government sources, Sisavang Vatthana was never crowned, and, after his exile in the north, he returned to Luang Prabang and resided in a private residence near Wat Sieng Thong, where the two legendary holy men had prophesied that a royal city would be built. At that time (the official reports claim) Sisavang Vatthana donated the royal palace to the Lao People's Democratic Republic.

*　　*　　*

The apparently permanent establishment of Vientiane as Laos's administrative capital in the twentieth century assured Luang Prabang's seclusion from the mainstream of the country's political and economic activities. When, in the 1960s, Osborne travelled the same route that the Lagrée party had taken a century before, of all the settlements along the Mekong, Luang Prabang was possibly the settlement that had changed the least since its first exploration (Osborne, 1969, p. 236). Even in 1995, Laos has no railroads, and the road that leads from Vientiane to Luang Prabang is unpaved and dusty, almost as inhospitable as the mighty river. Luang Prabang's population is about 8,000, roughly the same as Henri Mouhot estimated in 1861.

It is fascinating to compare Luang Prabang as it exists in the last decade of the twentieth century with nineteenth-century descriptions. Although boats from nearby villages still ply their way up and down the Mekong, the traffic is less congested than that noted by Garnier. The arbitrary boundaries, which, since the late nineteenth century, have separated northern Laos from Thailand, Burma, and China, have curtailed the lively trade that once crowded Luang Prabang's river-banks. Elephants crossing the Mekong near Luang Prabang are no longer a major means of transport: instead, a large bridge just south of Vientiane connects Laos with its former territories west of the river. And while vendors' stalls can still be found along Luang Prabang's river-banks, the city's main market has been moved to a large building south of Phu Si. Yet a stairway of several hundred steps still leads to Tat Chom Si at the summit of the hill, and the city's main avenue, along which Luang Prabang's royalty once paraded with pomp and splendour, still connects the esplanade at Tat Luang with Wat Sieng Thong at the confluence of the Mekong and the Nam Khan. There, a wide and imposing stairway still leads down the Mekong's river-bank, providing access to the city for travellers arriving by boat.

There are not as many *wat* as there used to be. In 1888 the French had counted forty-five monasteries, and in the early twentieth century, the French archaeologist, Louis Finot, documented thirty-four, about the same as in the late twentieth century. Brick and stucco have largely replaced the old wooden constructs

(Colour Plate 18), and the high pent roof seen in the old engraving of the *sim* at Wat Wisun is no longer in style.

Under French rule, Luang Prabang's secular architecture also was altered considerably. In the late nineteenth century, the city's first French residents had been delighted to live and work in large buildings built in the style of the local houses, supported high off the ground on pilings and surrounded by verandas (Pavie et al., Vol. 2, p. 32; Vol. 6, p. 47). Houses of wood, bamboo, and thatch (Colour Plate 19) have continued to crowd Luang Prabang's narrow, east–west lanes. But by the early twentieth century the French were hiring Vietnamese builders, and many of the old wooden buildings were covered with stucco. The lower storeys of these houses, once open to the outside, were often enclosed (Plate 29; Colour Plate 20); roofs of man-made material replaced those made of thatch; Vietnamese-style shop-houses became common along the main streets (Plate 30; Colour Plate 21). Luang Prabang's aristocracy began living in French colonial mansions built

29. A traditional house in Luang Prabang, with its lower storey enclosed. (Betty Gosling)

30. Twentieth-century Vietnamese-style shop-house. (Betty Gosling)

of brick instead of wood, and many of those are now public buildings (Colour Plate 22).

In 1904, with the aid of Vietnamese workers, the French began construction of the new royal palace, known as the Ho Kham, or Golden Hall, for the newly crowned king, Sisavang Vong (Plate 31). The former palace—which was not, in fact, so very old, since it had been entirely rebuilt after the Chinese destruction of the city in 1887—was a conglomeration of large, rambling houses made of wood and bamboo, raised, Lao-style, high off the ground on stilts. The imposing new building constructed of brick under the supervision of the French, was European. But, it was situated on the banks of the Mekong just west of the hill, Phu Si, next to where the old royal compound had once been located. Although, judging from nineteenth-century maps and photographs, the old royal compound had faced the confluence of the Mekong and Nam Khan, where the legendary holy men had prophesied the palace would be built, the new French building faced the sacred mount.

31. Ho Kham, or royal palace, with pediment depicting Luang Prabang's fifteen mythological *naga* and three-headed elephant. (Betty Gosling)

Important visitors could still arrive by river at the royal embarcadero, however, and mount the stairways that led to the palace grounds. And although King Sisavang Vong had studied in Paris and was the most European of all Luang Prabang's kings, he insisted that a pinnacle that covered the throne room of the new palace be replaced with one of Lao design. In the mid-twentieth century, in preparation for his coronation, King Sisavang Vatthana enlarged the building by adding a new room on either side of the old hall.

Now, in the late twentieth century, with kings no longer in residence, the palace functions as the country's national museum, 'the main aims of which are to preserve the palace and the royal collection and inform the public of the history of the former monarchy' (Thongsa, n.d.). Depicted on the pediment above the entrance, a three-headed elephant represents Indra's mount, Erawan, or alternately, Khun Borom's fabled elephant-mount, the royal emblem of old Lan Sang. More recently the three-headed elephant has acquired additional symbolism: the unification of three Lao kingdoms—Luang Prabang, Vientiane, and Champasak. But the old persists; surrounding the elephant, fifteen intertwining serpents recall the *naga* that so jealously guarded Luang Prabang's rivers and fields before the city was founded. In the museum one can still see the royal throne of the Lao kings, their gold and silver sabres, royal seals and medals, and the royal elephant chair on which the kings once rode in honorific splendour. Several of the palace rooms are still furnished as they were when the last kings resided there, and Buddha images that may have adorned the palace tables when the old king, Oun Kham, received Lagrée and his party in 1867 are still on display. Huge portraits of Sisavang Vatthana, Queen Kham Phui, and Crown Prince Vong Savang, painted by the Russian artist Ilya Glazunov in 1967, adorn the walls. And a large mural depicts scenes from the life of Khun Borom, the legendary founder of Luang Prabang's (and Laos's) royal dynasty.

Relics of Luang Prabang's religious past are also evident: the dais of the Supreme Patriarch of the Buddhist Order; the elephant tusks that Garnier had admired and described so enthusiastically at Wat Wisun; ornate temple carvings; and the crystal and gold Buddha images that were found when the Tat Makmo stupa at Wat Wisun collapsed during the 1887 invasion of the Chinese.

Efforts are under way to preserve other of Luang Prabang's treasures. At a conference on historic preservation held in Chiang Mai (Thailand) in January 1995, and sponsored by the Asia Society (New York) and the Siam Society (Bangkok), one of the most heated debates concerned the possible conversion of one of Luang Prabang's princely French colonial mansions into a hotel. Although the question was left unresolved, all of the city's thirty-three temple complexes have been listed by the National Heritage Foundation and Unesco (United Nations Educational, Scientific, and Cultural Organization) for preservation; and every wooden structure that predates the introduction of French and Vietnamese architecture is to be saved. The banks of the river are to be preserved, and it is hoped that commercialism will be kept in check.

Remnants of Luang Prabang's old monthly ceremonies persist. The April New Year's festival is a yearly occurrence, and the one held at Luang Prabang is the most lavish in all the country. But its nature has changed. The *devata luang*, Pu No and Na No, no longer take part, and the carnival atmosphere has disappeared: the event is identified primarily as a Buddhist holiday. Boat races, with a wide variety of symbolic meanings, are held at various times of the year at Luang Prabang and throughout the country. The Twelfth Month Festival, once the major royal ritual event in Luang Prabang's yearly calendar, is now celebrated only in the country's administrative capital, Vientiane. The ceremonies reflect the accomplishments of a government that is no longer royal.

In spite of conflicts, invasions, and the dramatic and traumatic changes that have befallen Luang Prabang's neighbours, the city retains its Arcadian charm. Monks in saffron robes stroll the courtyards of their temples, study their texts, and maintain their temple grounds. The dome of verdure, the sacred hill, Phu Si, surmounted by Tat Chom Si, remains the focal point of the city, and the reddish roofs of the Buddhist monasteries still contrast with the deep green of the vegetation. During the dry season, one can see the boulders where *naga* repose during their yearly migrations to and from the rice-fields.

And what of the Pra Bang, the palladium of the kingdom, which for six centuries protected the land and its people and on which the country depended for its survival? Despite the radical changes in Laos's political structure and regardless of the devastations and the conflicts of the past, the Pra Bang endures. The royal statue (or, perhaps, a copy—the symbolism remains) now resides in princely splendour in a room to the right of the main entrance of the royal palace-turned-museum, and an imposing new *sim* in which the Pra Bang will be permanently installed is being built at the front of the palace grounds. Although no king has reigned in Laos for several decades, Luang Prabang is still recognized as the home of Laos's founding monarchs and the birthplace of a united Laos. The Pra Bang, the royal city, and the country have survived.

Appendix

Kings of Laos

Khun Borom. Mythological ancestor of the kings of Lan Sang (later known as Laos), said to have descended from the heavenly regions at Muang Then.

Khun Lo. Son of Khun Borom, and according to the annals of Lan Sang, the first king of Luang Prabang.

Chanthapanit. According to local annals, a humble betel merchant who became Luang Prabang's first king.

Fa Ngum. Lan Sang's—and Luang Prabang's—first historically documented king, who ruled from 1353 until 1373.

Sam Saen Tai. Son of Fa Ngum. Ruled from 1373 until 1416.

Numerous kings with short reigns. Fifteenth century. (Unnamed in the text.)

Wisun. Ruled from Luang Prabang, 1501–20.

Photthisarat. Ruled from Luang Prabang, 1520–7; from Vientiane, 1527–47.

Setthathirat. Ruled from Luang Prabang, 1548–63; from Vientiane, 1563–71. Prior to his reign at Luang Prabang, Setthathirat ruled Lan Na from Chiang Mai.

Laotian kings ruling from Vientiane, 1563–1707. Not mentioned in the text.

Kings ruling concurrently from Vientiane, Luang Prabang, and Champasak, 1707–1851. Not discussed in the text.

Tiantha. Ruled under Siamese supervision at Luang Prabang, 1851–72.

Oun Kham. Ruled under Siamese supervision from Luang Prabang, 1872–93; under French protection, 1893–4.

Sakkalin. Ruled under French protection from Luang Prabang, 1894–1904.

Sisavang Vong. Ruled under French protection from Luang Prabang, 1904–47; under constitutional monarchy, 1947–59.

Sisavang Vatthana. Ruled from Luang Prabang, 1959–75; under constitutional monarchy.

Glossary

Angkor. Capital of the Khmer, or Angkorian, Empire from 802 until *c*.1440.

Angkor Wat. Major temple at Angkor, built *c*.1100.

Annam. Former kingdom in what is now southern Vietnam.

Asoka. Powerful Buddhist king who ruled India in the third century BC.

Bang fai. Ceremonial rocket.

Bangkok. Capital of Siam (Thailand) from 1782 to the present.

Betel. Indian pepper plant, the leaves of which, mixed with areca nuts and other ingredients, are chewed for enjoyment. Betel often refers to the mixture.

Bodhi tree. The tree (*Ficus religiosa*) under which the Buddha meditated at Bodhi Gaya, India, just prior to his enlightenment. Slips of the tree are said to have been transported to many places throughout South Asia, where they were planted in Theravada monastery compounds.

Brahmin. Member of the highest, or priestly, Hindu caste.

Buddha. Founder of the Buddhist religion who lived in India in the sixth century BC.

Buddhism. Indian religious system based on the teachings of the Buddha, which took many forms as it spread throughout Asia. *See also Mahayana* and *Theravada.*

Champasak. In the eighteenth century an independent Lao kingdom in what is now southern Laos.

Chiang Mai. Capital city of Lan Na in what is now northern Thailand.

Cochin-China. Region in south-central Vietnam.

Delaporte, Louis. Artist who travelled with the Lagrée–Garnier French Mekong expedition.

Deva. Minor Buddhist deity.

Devata. Buddhist tutelary deity.

Devata luang. Buddhist term for the major tutelary deity (*phi muang*) of a city-state, or *muang.*

Dok so fa. Metal device symbolizing the universe placed on the roof of Lao *sim.*

Erawan. The 33-headed elephant-mount of the god Indra and the national symbol of Laos. Erawan is usually depicted with only three heads.

Garnier, Francis. French naval officer second-in-command of the Mekong expedition of 1866–8.

Hanglin. Bamboo or wooden device by means of which holy water is poured over an image of the Buddha.

Hinduism. Ancient polytheistic religion of India, practised in certain places in South-East Asia; the state religion of the Khmer Empire throughout most of its history.

Indo-China. A general term referring to Laos, Vietnam, and Cambodia; sometimes, Siam.

Indra. Major Hindu god incorporated into Theravada Buddhism as the king of the gods.

Kha. Aboriginal people who inhabited Laos before the arrival of the Lao.

Khmer Empire. A powerful empire centred at Angkor, in what is now southern Cambodia, which, at times, controlled much of mainland South-East Asia.

Lagrée, Doudart de. Naval officer and organizer and leader of the French Mekong expedition of 1866–8.

Lan Na. Land of the Million Rice Fields. From the thirteenth to the eighteenth century, a kingdom in what is now northern Thailand.

Lan Sang. Land of the Million Elephants. Former name of Laos, or the Lao People's Democratic Republic.

Lao. A branch of the Tai-speaking family that settled in what is now Laos.

Lao People's Democratic Republic. Since 1975, the official name of Laos.

Laotian. Pertaining to the people and country of Laos.

Lefèvre-Pontalis, Pierre. Assistant to the chief of the French Mission at Luang Prabang.

Lolo. Tibeto-Burman linguistic group of south-western China.

Lu. Tai linguistic group inhabiting south-west China and northern Burma, Thailand, and Laos.

Mahayana. Branch of Buddhism adopted by the peoples of northern Asia and in the twelfth and thirteenth centuries by the Khmer Empire.

Meo. Old name for *Hmong*, Tai-speaking linguistic group inhabiting parts of south-western China and northern areas of Thailand, Laos, and Vietnam.

Mongkut. See Rama IV.

Mouhot, Henri. French naturalist credited with the European discovery of Angkor Wat; the first European known to visit Luang Prabang.

Muang. A Tai principality or city-state; also, the city at the centre of the principality.

Muang Sawa. Old name for the area that would later be called Luang Prabang.

Muang Then. Old name for Dien Bien Phu. According to Lao mythology and twentieth-century linguists, the birthplace of the Tai people.

Na No. One of Lang Sang's two *devata luang*, formerly a servant of Khun Borom, mythological king of Lang Sang.

Naga. Serpent deity.

Nirvana. In Buddhist thought, the release from earthly bonds.

Pagoda. French term for *sim*.

Pali. Indic language in which Theravada texts are written.

Pathet Lao. Communist forces that gained control of the Laotian government in 1975.

Pavie, Auguste. The first French diplomat stationed at Luang Prabang; under French rule, Laos's first governor-general.

Phi. Member of the Tai spirit world.

Phi luang. Chief guardian spirit of a *muang. See also devata luang.*

Phu Si. Sacred hill. The mount at the centre of Luang Prabang.

Pra. Honorific term applied to esteemed persons and sacred objects.

Pra Bang. Image of the Buddha that is the palladium of Laos.

Pra Keo. Image of the Buddha respected as the palladium of Thailand.

Prasat. A palace or palace-like structure; the small edifice in which the Pra Bang was placed on ceremonial occasions.

Pu No. One of Lang Sang's two *devata luang*, formerly a servant of Khun Borom, mythological king of Lan Sang.

Punkah. Large swinging screen-like fan hung from the ceiling and moved by ropes.

Rama I. King of Siam from 1782 to 1809.

Rama III. King of Siam from 1824 to 1851.

Rama IV. King of Siam from 1851 to 1868.

Sampot. In Cambodian dress, a wide piece of fabric wrapped around the hips, knotted in front, passed between the legs, and attached at the back to the belt.

Satou. The abbot of a Lao Theravada monastery.

Siam. Large area west of Laos ruled from Bangkok; old name for Thailand.

Siamese. Tai people who settled in what is now Thailand.

Sieng. Lao and northern Thai equivalent of *muang*, or city-state.

Sieng Dong-Sieng Thong. Old name of Luang Prabang.

Sim. Congregation hall in a Lao Theravada Buddhist monastery

Sinhalese. Pertaining to Sri Lanka and its people.

Sip Song Phan Na. Land of the Twelve Thousand Rice Fields. Area in southern Yunnan, China, now known as Xishuangbanna; at one time an independent principality, sometimes ruled by Laos.

Sri Lanka. Island kingdom in the Indian Ocean, also known as Ceylon. In the third century BC, Buddhism spread from India to Ceylon, where the tenets of the Theravada religion were formulated.

Stupa. Buddhist reliquary monument.

Sukhothai. In the late thirteenth and fourteenth centuries, the largest and most powerful *muang* in what is now central Thailand.

Tai. A large linguistic group including the Thai and Lao.

Taksin. King of Siam who ruled Thonburi from 1767 to 1782.

Tat. Lao term for stupa.

Theravada. The most conservative branch of Buddhism, which spread from Sri Lanka throughout South-East Asia in the thirteenth century AD.

Thonburi. Capital of Siam from 1767 to 1782.

Tonkin. Northern region of Vietnam.

Tripitaka. Collection of texts that make up the Theravada Buddhist canon.

Vientiane. City in central Laos that has alternated with Luang Prabang as the country's capital. The present-day administrative capital of Laos.

Wat. Lao or Thai Theravada Buddhist monastery.

Bibliography

About Laos (1958), Washington, DC: Royal Embassy of Laos Press and Information Service.

Archaimbault, Charles (1972), *La course de pirogues au Laos: un complexe culturel*, *Artibus Asiae*, Ascona (Switzerland): Artibus Asiae Publishers, Supplementum 29, pp. 11–120.

――――― (1973), *Structures religieuses lao (rites et mythes)*, Vientiane: Editions Vithagna.

Berval, René de (ed.) (1959), *Kingdom of Laos: The Land of the Million Elephants and of the White Parasol*, Saigon: France–Asie.

Boudet, Paul and Masson, André (1931), *Iconographie historique de l'Indochine Française*, Paris: Les Editions G. Van Oest.

Condominas, Georges (1975), 'Phiban Cults in Rural Laos', in G. W. Skinner and A. T. Kirsch (eds.), *Change and Persistence in Thai Society: Essays in Honor of Lauriston Sharp*, Ithaca, New York: Cornell University Press, pp. 252–73.

Cummings, Joe (1994), *Laos: A Travel Survival Kit*, Berkeley: Lonely Planet Publications.

Devillers, Philippe (1970), 'The Laotian Conflict in Perspective', in Nina S. Adams and Alfred W. McCoy (eds.), *Laos: War and Revolution*, New York: Harper and Row, pp. 37–51.

Deydier, Henri (1954), *Lokapāla: génies, totems et sorciers du nord Laos*, Paris: Librairie Plon.

Finot, Louis (1917), *Recherches sur la litterature laotienne*, *Bulletin de l'École Française d'Extrême-Orient*, Vol. 17, No. 5.

Flood, Chadin (trans.) (1966), *The Dynastic Chronicles, Bangkok Era, the Fourth Reign*, Tokyo: Centre for East Asian Cultural Studies, Vol. 2.

Flood, Thadeus and Flood, Chadin (eds., trans.) (1978), *The Dynastic Chronicles, Bangkok Era, the First Reign*, Tokyo: Centre for East Asian Cultural Studies, Vol. 1.

The French in Indo-China (1884), London: T. Nelson and Sons.

Garnier, Francis (1873), *Voyage d'exploration en Indo-Chine effectué pendant les années 1866, 1867, et 1868*, Paris: Librairie Hachette, 2 vols.

Griswold, A. B. and Prasert na Nagara (1971), 'Epigraphic and Historical Studies No. 9: The Inscription of Ramagamhaeng of Sukhodaya

(1292 A.D.)', *Journal of the Siam Society,* Vol. 59, No. 2, pp. 179–228.

Hall, D. G. E. (1964), *A History of South-East Asia,* New York: Macmillan.

LeBar, Frank M. and Suddard, Adrienne (1960), *Laos: Its People, Its Society, Its Culture,* New Haven: Hraf Press.

Le Boulanger, Paul (1934), *Histoire du Laos française,* Paris: Librairie Plon.

Le Laos (1967), *La Revue Française de l'Élite Européenne,* No. 203.

Levy, Paul (1940), 'Les traces de l'introduction du Bouddhism a Luang Prabang', *Bulletin de l'École Française d'Extrême-Orient,* Vol. 40, pp. 411–28.

Lingat, R. (1934), 'Le culte du Bouddha d'Émeraude', *Journal of the Siam Society,* Vol. 27, No. 1, pp. 9–38.

Marchal, Henri (1964), 'L'art décoratif au Laos', *Arts Asiatiques,* Vol. 10, No. 2.

McCoy, Alfred W. (1970), 'French Colonialism in Laos: 1893–1945', in Nina S. Adams and Alfred W. McCoy (eds.), *Laos: War and Revolution,* New York: Harper and Row, pp. 67–99.

Mouhot, M. Henri (1864), *Travels in the Central Parts of Indo-China (Siam), Cambodia, and Laos, during the Years 1858, 1859, and 1860,* London: John Murray, Vol. 2.

Osborne, Milton (1969), *River Road to China: The Mekong River Expedition of 1866–1873,* New York: Liveright.

Pallegoix, Jean-Baptiste (1854), *Royaume Thai ou Siam,* Paris: Mission de Siam, Vol. 1.

Parmentier, Henri (1954), *L'art du Laos, Publications de l'École Française d'Extrême Orient,* Vol. 35.

Pavie, Auguste (1898), *Mission Pavie: Études diverses, Recherches sur l'histoire du Cambodge, du Laos et du Siam,* Paris: Ernest Leroux, Vol. 2.

Pavie, Auguste; Lefèvre-Pontalis, Pierre; and Captains Cupet, Malglaive, and de Rivière (1900–19), *Mission Pavie Indo-Chine, 1879–1895: géographie et voyages,* Paris: Ernest Leroux, 7 vols.

Raquez, A. (1902), *Pages laotiennes,* Hanoi: F. H. Schneider.

Reinach, Lucien de (1911), *Le Laos,* Paris: Librairie Orientale et Américaine.

Renaud, Jean (1930), *Le Laos: dieux, bonzes, et montagnes,* Paris: A. Redier.

Reynolds, Frank E. (1978), 'Ritual and Social Hierarchy: An Aspect of Traditional Religion in Buddhist Laos', in Bardwell L. Smith (ed.), *Religion and Legitimation of Power in Thailand, Laos, and Burma,* Chambersburg, Pennsylvania: Anima Books, pp. 166–74.

Sarraut, Albert (1930), *Indochine,* Paris: Librairie de Paris, Firmen-Didot.

Thongsa Sayavongkhamdy (n.d.), *Ho Kham: Guide to the Royal Palace, Luang Prabang,* Vientiane: Ministry of Information and Culture.

Whitmore, John K. (1970), 'The Thai-Vietnamese Struggle for Laos in the Nineteenth Century', in Nina S. Adams and Alfred W. McCoy (eds.), *Laos: War and Revolution*, New York: Harper and Row, pp. 53–66.

Wyatt, David K. (1982), *Thailand: A Short History*, New Haven: Yale University Press.

Zago, Marcel (1972), *Rites et ceremonies en milieu bouddhiste Lao*, Rome: Università Gregoriana Editrice.

Index

References in brackets refer to Plate numbers; those in brackets and italics to Colour Plate numbers.